COMMON
SENSE
IN
CLASSROOM
RELATIONS

COMMON
SENSE
IN
CLASSROOM
RELATIONS

ROBERT SYLWESTER
CONCORDIA TEACHERS COLLEGE

Parker Publishing Co., Inc.
West Nyack, N.Y.

Fifth printing .... April, 1969

PRINTED IN THE UNITED STATES OF AMERICA

15275–B & P

A PRACTICAL APPROACH
TO CLASSROOM RELATIONSHIPS

The development and maintenance of good classroom relationships is generally the most compelling problem elementary and junior high teachers face. Inexperienced teachers rarely achieve complete success, and even experienced teachers must constantly work to maintain the level of achievement expected of them.

Your pupils look to you for a model of a successful adult. By living and working with many adults during their growing years, they develop convictions about group living that help them establish the social patterns of their lives. In your role of teacher, it is important that you introduce your pupils to those social values society wants explored in school. This book will show you how to do this effectively.

The development of self-evaluation and self-discipline abilities are major goals in the area of human relationships. The best way to develop these abilities in pupils is to demonstrate them in your own conduct as you work with your class to solve the many problems that arise in your classroom during the school year. This book will show you how to help pupils act properly on the basis of a careful evalution of the situation, and thus move closer to maturity.

Common Sense in Classroom Relations approaches classroom human relations through fifty-seven problem areas that teachers and pupils face as they work together from September to June. It explores the special human relations problems that occur in the beginning of the school year when the class is getting acquainted, during the middle of the year when they grow as a group, and at the end of the year when they have matured as much as they will mature as a group. This book proposes practical solutions to these problems within the context of limitations imposed by the nature and purpose of formal education in our society, by space and time restrictions that exist in schools, by the immaturity of pupils, and by the different values and expectations teachers and pupils often hold.

7

To be effective, suggestions for solving human relations problems must develop respect, affection, and courtesy, qualities that exist in groups that work together effectively. The ideas suggested in this book will encourage the developmeint of these qualities in your class. In many instances, you can use the suggestions as presented. In other cases, you will develop variations to fit your particular school situation. In either case, though, you should find this book a particular resource with which to examine the human relations problems you face in your work as a teacher.

Most people act on the basis of theories of living they hold. The pupils you work with can only know your convictions about life through your behavior. You communicate your convictions about human relations through your handling of human relations problems that arise in your class. It is important that you communicate clearly to the class what you believe, and that you believe what you communicate. Consequently, the book is a practical approach to classroom relationships. Theories that underlie it are communicated through the activities it suggests.

Most effective procedures for dealing with classroom problems are basically simple so that they do communicate meaning clearly. They also contain that element best called common sense. I trust you will find this to be the case with the ideas and activities that follow.

ROBERT SYLWESTER
SEWARD, NEBRASKA

CONTENTS

PART III:
AT THE END

PART I:
AT THE BEGINNING

1

PREPARE PROPERLY
FOR THE SCHOOL YEAR

BEGIN WITH BASIC PRINCIPLES

Successful teachers are at least one step ahead of their pupils. They begin thinking seriously about school while their pupils are still romping in the sun. During the pre-school weeks they study themselves, records of pupils they will work with, and the community in which they will work. They set goals on the basis of principles that govern group behavior, and since goals can be implemented in many different ways, they begin to plan activities that will challenge the specific group they will teach. Begin your year by thinking through again what it means to work with a classroom full of pupils.

Your class is a formal group since membership is assigned and because it exists as a group for a specified time. It will be similar to other groups drawn from the same general population so you will be able to transfer knowledge and experience you have gained from previous classes, but it will also be a unique group in that no other group in existence is exactly like it.

It will mature sequentially as a group. First meetings will produce an impression of sorts that will be strengthened or altered in successive meetings through the year. What occurs on any day cannot be undone. You and your class can only build on what has occurred and continue to grow in patience and tolerance with each other.

This implies that you should work to develop a feeling of acceptance in the group. Each person should be accepted for what he is in September and for what he can be the following June. Such growth will come only when members feel free to express their real feelings about each other, but strive to do so pleasantly and charitably.

While the development of good human relations is the responsibility of every member of your class, you bear a special responsibility to structure and order class activities so that good human relations are fostered. As the most mature person in your room, you must be prepared to exhibit patience, love, understanding and leadership; to give and give with little thought of return.

ASSESS YOURSELF HONESTLY

You will be with your pupils about a thousand hours during the school year. During this period they will examine you very closely. Many will spend more time with you than with any other adult. Will they see an adult worthy of emulation? Is the teacher who is trying to instill scholarship in them a scholar himself? Does the teacher who tries to teach them how to live with others get along with his fellow teachers? Is the one adult in the classroom the most mature person in the room? How will you fare during a thousand hour examination?

Our society places three classes of adults in schoolrooms. The first group does little more than guard the premises and keep pupils from committing mayhem on each other. They help pupils fulfill compulsory attendance requirement. They know little and teach less. They got their jobs because competent teachers were not readily available at the time. Fortunately, there are relatively few of these, but even one in a school is too many.

The second class comprises the majority of people holding teaching positions. They fill students' minds. They have a college degree and they have mastered the rudiments of teaching. They teach the ABC's, the state capitals, and the periodic tables when the course of study says they should. Their record in developing good classroom relationships is usually acceptable but not often outstanding. The word competent best describes them as teachers. Many would be more than this, but their vision of teaching is limited. Many could be more than this, but family and other outside school interests and responsibilities sap their time and energy.

The third class is worthy of the name teacher. They move students' minds. Facts stored up in students' minds during previous years are moved around and organized for effective use during the year they teach. They relate items of information to major generalizations. They develop in students a deeper understanding of such ideas as patience, love, tolerance, and acceptance. These teachers create another teacher in the mind of each student, a teacher who takes over at the end of the year and continues to goad the student throughout his life. Most of us can remember three or four such teachers. Each school has a few and everyone knows who they are, even though they come in a variety of personalities, body types, and ages.

As you prepare to begin the school year, consider the following traits often associated with successful teaching. The third class of teacher described above would answer yes to each of these questions. Where you have to answer no, take steps to improve yourself.

Do you have an essentially positive view of yourself? If you do, you would have to grant honestly that, as others get to know you, they like you. You would admit that you continue to increase measurably in effectiveness as a teacher and as a human being with each passing year. You know your profession well enough to deal adequately with most problems that face you. You know what you can handle yourself and what you should refer to others. You have confidence in your ability to make decisions when you must make them. You are not afraid to try new ideas. You are willing to argue and work for the acceptance of your ideas and convictions.

Do you have strong compassionate feeling for your fellow man? If you do, you accept others for what they are, and you accept them emotionally as well as intellectually. You sense how things seem to the other fellow. You show a deep respect for the dignity and integrity of each person you meet. You are willing to give deeply of yourself with little thought of return. You love those who are antagonistic to you.

Do you love learning? If you do, you can point to books you purchased within the year, to magazines and newspapers you read

regularly, to concerts and plays and lectures you attended, to significant TV programs you saw, to a frequently used library card. No
teacher can teach more than he knows. Few can teach as much as they
know. But the more a teacher knows, the greater is his potential for
teaching. Good teachers know a lot. They have an enthusiasm for
learning that they want to pass on to others.

Do you work at teaching? If you do, you can point to carefully
developed and organized plans for the classes you teach, to well-
organized files of teaching materials you have gathered and used
through the years, to effort and hours beyond your contractual obligations. Good teachers improvise during the school day as they seize on
opportunities to follow along paths their students want to explore, but
such improvisation is a deliberate choice between a carefully planned
lesson and a more promising new direction. Classes are not met cold in
the hope that the students will suggest the direction the period should
take. Poor teachers have a tendency to moan about class misbehavior.
Good teachers go about their way planning challenging lessons. They
know that the quality of activity at the front of the room determines
the quantity of activity in the aisles.

Can you laugh at yourself? If you can, you can point to several
things that indicate you don't take yourself too seriously. You don't
burden your class with a number of fussy rules and regulations that
exist purely or primarily because the behavior in question annoys you,
although it doesn't unduly bother other teachers. You don't bristle
defensively when you hear jokes about teachers. Pupils find it easy to
talk with you informally and you find it easy to talk informally with
them. You're willing to admit you don't know the answer to a question
if you don't know it. You'll admit you made a mistake on something
instead of trying to weasel out of your predicament. You have the
capacity to see the light side of most things that occur. You are relaxed
when you are around people.

Suppose you answered no to one or more of the above questions.
Reread the paragraph following it carefully to find the specific cause of
your problem. Then write out your own thoughts and reactions to the
situation in a paragraph or two. Feel free to agree or disagree with the
statements made in this book, but write out your thoughts, don't just

think about them. If you're relatively normal, and chances are you are, you should be able to begin working out some solution to your problem once you see it in writing, especially if you put your paragraph aside for a few days before considering it. Move toward a solution as your personality and ability dictate. Each of these characteristics can be acquired by any teacher willing to expend the effort. Try it. It is difficult because self-scrutiny is difficult. That's why most people avoid it. As a teacher, though, you can't afford to avoid it. Too many pupils watch you work. Too many pupils are dependent on you as a model of a successful adult.

GET ACQUAINTED WITH THE COMMUNITY

Teaching is a mobile profession. By chance or design many teachers teach away from their home communities. Indeed some teachers don't feel at home in communities where they have worked for years.

I attended college almost 2,000 miles from home. During the first few weeks, I tried to move a large West Coast city, the mountains, and the Pacific Ocean into a small Midwest town surrounded by cornfields. My unfavorable comments and comparisons in dorm discussions progressively antagonized those who lived with me. One day it went too far. I was told in no uncertain terms that the whole group would be happy to help me pack and catch the next train west. If I didn't need the Midwest, it certainly didn't need me. I had never been so embarrassed. With no place to turn, I swallowed my pride, settled down, and discovered that small towns can be quite pleasant, that leaving one's childhood home is a part of growing up.

The community that provides you with a monthly paycheck is home to your pupils. It's your home too as long as you live there. Start getting acquainted with it before you start to teach in it, and continue to study it as long as you live in it.

Listen to the people. Start conversations with them in stores and in the street, in parks and at church. Talk with salespeople when you shop. Listen unobtrusively while you're waiting with others at traffic signals, at bus stops, in theater lines. Listen to children especially. Watch them at play in the parks. Get to know your paperboy. What sort of children live in your community?

Read the signs that tell about a community. How is the major shopping district maintained? What sort of entertainment thrives? Are homes and yards kept up? Is the community justly proud of its libraries, museums, parks, and historical shrines? Are the industrial and business leaders of the community interested in the welfare of their employees and vice versa? Are municipal services adequate? Do people tend to speak of their community with pride or in criticism? What happens to community improvement issues on the ballot?

Become acquainted with the local communications media. Subscribe to the local papers. Watch local TV programs. The Chamber of Commerce in most larger communities issues publications periodically. Get on their mailing list. Several gasoline companies issue travel booklets describing accommodations and highlights of the various communities in a region. Purchase one that describes your region.

As you become acquainted with your community look for ways to bring it into your classroom. Visit field trip possibilities during the pre-school weeks. Meet potential resource people. Look for ways to correlate the history, industry, and culture of the region with your teaching.

You must take the initiative in getting acquainted. Most people are too caught up in their own lives to be overly concerned with new-comers. One good way to get acquainted is to join a community organization that is concerned with something close to your heart. Let that contact lead you to others. It's easy for teachers to cut themselves off from such contacts because of the demands of their work. Resist such temptations. It's not good for an adult to live in a world in which most of his interpersonal contact is with children. All adults need the stimulation of other adults on an informal avocational basis. You work with children. Live with adults.

If you accept a teaching position in your home community, many of the problems described above may not concern you. On the other hand, you will probably face other problems. Foremost among these may be your inability to view your community as objectively as a teacher should. For example, you may harbor conscious or unconscious biases against business and community leaders through some family difficulty that occurred during your childhood. You may be biased towards entire sections of town because of strong athletic rivalries that existed during your high school years. You may oversimplify and even romanticize complex community problems because your acquaintance with these problems stems from your childhood. It's difficult to be unemotional about urban renewal in areas where we played as children.

Deliberately re-examine your home community when you make the move from private citizen to public servant. Revisit places you last visited as a child. Restudy community problems. Re-examine libraries and museums. As you re-acquaint yourself with your community, approach it from your new perspective as a professional teacher who loves his community enough to return to it, but who also realizes that he must now view it objectively as well as subjectively and not permit personal bias to color his school time comments on his community.

Ask yourself why you returned. What does your community contain that is good, that should be developed even more? What is the potential of your community? How can you as a teacher help improve your community? Ask youself what would have drawn you elsewhere had you not returned to your home town. What can you as a teacher do to rectify community weaknesses? Since you attended school in this community you should be able to recall ways in which your teachers made you aware of your community's strengths and weaknesses. And you should be able to recall opportunities they let slip by. Begin to plan activities that will make your pupils conscious of their community and proud to be a part of it. Become active in community affairs that are consistent with your interests, whether these be recreational, musical, political, or avocational. Make a deliberate attempt through such activities to expand your circle of friendships beyond the people you have known most of your life.

MEET YOUR CO-WORKERS

Many teachers are apprehensive about joining a school staff and meeting the established faculty. The returning teachers are already acquainted with each other and with the policies and procedures that govern their work. They form an in-group of sorts that can cause concern to a new teacher. Some of this apprehension revolves around the fear of making a poor impression, of saying the wrong thing at the wrong time, of forgetting names, of forgetting assigned responsibilities. If these things concern you, it might help your peace of mind to recall a few facets of human nature.

The best way to make a good impression is to put the other person at ease. He doesn't know what to expect either. You put another person at ease by smiling easily, by saying hello, by picking up any conversational gambits tossed out, by dressing conservatively, by asking for help and advice, and by doing countless other things that cast the spotlight on the other person and make him look good. We are always impressed by those who seem impressed by us.

The best way to say the right thing at the right time when you are new in a group is to listen to the other person talk and ask intelligent questions once in a while. It's not good to begin a cordial relationship with a controversial topic. Wait till you know the other person well enough to speak frankly with him. This isn't cowardice. It's just good sense. There will be time enough to discuss all issues during the year. The order in which they are discussed is rarely so important that you can't begin with such topics as the weather and move on from there. Don't get involved in gripe sessions early in the year (if ever). Listen if you must, but don't talk. You'll probably regret anything you say.

People who remember names well usually work at it. They develop little memory aids that help fix names in their mind. They tend to use the person's name several times during their initial conversation. They examine the person they are meeting for any characteristics that can serve as an aid to remembering the person's name. You might carry a small notebook with you early in the year and jot down names and identifying characteristics of people you meet. Don't panic if you forget someone's name. Most people realize that newcomers have many more names to learn than the returning teachers. If you forget someone's name, apologize with a smile, and ask for it again. That's much better than trying to carry on a conversation with half your mind occupied searching for a name.

Make a special attempt to become acquainted with consultants and other administrative personnel. By and large, your problems define their task during the early months of the school year. They will be more than happy to explain again policies and procedures that you didn't completely understand or remember during the interminable consecutive meetings you attended during the pre-school workshop.

Meet any teachers who will be working with your pupils during the year. These include teachers who work with your entire class in such areas as physical education, art, or music, and teachers who work with individual pupils in such areas as speech and remedial reading. Discuss their work with them particularly as it relates to your schedule and to special class problems that can arise because of their work. These teachers can usually give you some pretty sensible advice about how to introduce them and their work to your class.

Introduce yourself to the custodian and secretary and to other noncertified personnel on the staff. They appreciate the opportunity to discuss their work with teachers and to suggest ways in which they can work efficiently and effectively with you.

If you are a returning teacher, do all you can to minimize the problems outlined above. Remember to mention your name the first five or six times you meet new teachers, to drop in to meet them and help them get started, to take them to coffee during the pre-school work days, to introduce them to other teachers, and to include them in your conversations, and to keep such conversations on a positive note. In short, think back to the time you were new to the school and do what you hoped others would do to you to make you feel accepted.

EXAMINE PUPIL RECORDS

You will first meet your pupils and their former teachers in the file folders where records are kept. Properly interpreted and used, these records can help fuse one year into the next with a minimum of wasted effort. Interpreting pupil records is difficult because such a vast amount of information has been reduced to a few words, letters and numbers. Just what does a "B" mean? Because definitions differ, records are often misinterpreted or ignored. This is unfortunate since the descriptions and evaluations summarized in a pupil's record were placed there because former teachers thought them important. You can gain much from a careful pre-school examination of pupil records if you will follow a few simple procedures.

Seek patterns. Patterns of evaluations mean much more than the individual comments and grades. If most former teachers commented that a pupil seemed unhappy much of the time, you might anticipate the same problem. But if one teacher commented that this was not the case during the year he knew the pupil, this deviation from a pattern would also be worth noting. In either case move to a second procedure.

Seek clarification. With a little effort you should be able to talk with former teachers of many of your pupils before school begins. They will be able to attach additional meaning to problems they summarized with a word or letter. Go prepared to ask specific questions so you won't waste their time needlessly. Minutes spent in such pre-school conferences can save hours later in the year.

Don't discount completely the evaluations of teachers who see things much differently than other teachers, and whose entries deviate sharply from other teachers' entries. These are the teachers who see sweetness and light in everything and everybody, or evil in everything and everybody. If many of your pupils had such a teacher the preceding year, you had better find out what he believes about children and teaching, because you're going to have to bring those pupils back to reality. Average pupils who received a flock of A's last year aren't going to take kindly to a return to realistic evaluations. Pupils who lived in an atmosphere of class tension last year will be a little leery of their new teacher this year. Seek such teachers out. Don't argue procedures with them. There's no need to antagonize colleagues this early in the year. Just ask questions and listen to their answers. Then quietly make your plans for a smooth transition from one approach to teaching to another.

Other people can also give you information on your prospective pupils. Many principals are proud of their extensive knowledge of their pupils. The school nurse is generally well acquainted with pupils who have problems. While care must be exercised in bending the ears of custodians, cooks, and secretaries, their comments on pupils in general are often revealing. They have the opportunity to observe behavior without responsibility for decision. Use good judgment in evaluating all such information and opinion.

A word of caution is in order at this point. While paper knowledge and even teacher-to-teacher knowledge of pupils is often revealing and generally valuable, it is important that you gather this information in the spirit of inquiry and not in terms of pre-school evaluation. You owe it to your pupils to hold off judgments on them until you have had a good opportunity to meet them and to work with them sufficiently to draw your own conclusions about their strengths and weaknesses. You will certainly want your superiors to show you that courtesy when they evaluate you and your work. It would come with ill grace for you not to show the same consideration to your pupils.

As you gather information on your prospective pupils, don't try to remember it all—because you can't. Write it down and begin a set of personal records that you will use through the year. Figure 1 illustrates one type that you might find useful. A separate form is used for each of

SUBJECT: HOME CONDITIONS

NAME	NO IMMEDIATE APPARENT PROBLEM	POTENTIAL PROBLEM	PROBLEM SITUATION
BILLY GREEN		*Both parents work. Father is traveling salesman. His work is erratic*	
MARY JONES	*Seems happy. Stable home. Parents interested in children. Adequate income.*		
FRANK ROSE			
BETTY SMITH			*Father dead. Mother remarried but separated from present husband. Housing poor. Mother works nights.*
ALFRED STARP	*Presently good →*	*He says his paternal grandfather is coming to live with them in a month. (Grandmother died recently.)*	

Figure 1.

several traits you wish to study, such as: Intellectual Status, Physical Condition, Social Status, Social Adjustment, General Emotional Status, Presence of Fears, Self-Concept, Attitude toward School, Classroom Behavior, Study Habits, Home Conditions. Many such classifications can be used.

You will not be able to fill out the forms completely before school begins. Indeed you will not have files on transfer pupils. The purpose of a pre-school beginning is to make sure you get started. You'll be far too busy to start once school begins, but it will be relatively easy to continue a practice already begun. Make entries with a pencil so they can be changed as conditions warrant. Don't be afraid to make a judgment for fear it will be wrong. It can always be changed when you discover your error. Don't forget to re-evaluate entries in the No Immediate Apparent Problem column frequently. Seek patterns in entries. Note which column received the most entries. Is there a pattern in the reasons advanced? What can you do about it in your teaching? What plans can you make before the school year begins?

Imagine meeting a class cold, then imagine meeting a class with a considerable amount of information about many of the students. It's well worth the effort.

SET TENTATIVE GOALS

When a community invests thousands and thousands of dollars in its schools, it wants to know what will go on inside. It expects teachers to state clearly and concisely what they plan to teach. That's what objectives are all about. Develop your general objectives for the year before the school year begins. You won't have to start from scratch. State and local curriculum guides and teachers' manuals for textbooks will give you good general suggestions that you can adapt to your particular teaching situation. But get them down in writing even if you have to refine them later after you meet your pupils and discover that some of your goals were unrealistic.

State objectives clearly in terms of things you expect pupils to do at the end of the year that they couldn't do at the beginning. For example, if they are to learn the multiplication tables during the year, you could state that specific objective in terms such as these: The pupils will be able to state orally or in writing all the 100 multiplication facts from one through ten. No doubt about what's meant by that objective. It's no crime for individual pupils to fail to meet or to go beyond the objective. Suppose only half the class masters the tables during the year, or suppose most master them by the middle of February. You will then be in a position either to re-evaluate your objective or else to change your teaching procedures the following year.

It's easier to write objectives about the multiplication tables than it is to write objectives about classroom human relations. Human relations aren't covered completely and clearly in teachers' guides either, and they involve a different set of considerations than more academic aspects of the curriculum. You should be able to write clear objectives about classroom relationships, however, if the behaviors that arise out of pupils' attitudes toward the teacher and each other can be clearly observed. And they can.

School human relations involves three areas: The relation of the school and its pupils to the community, the relation between pupils and staff, the relation among pupils. Let's examine each of these in terms of the major objective of the school as it deals with each of these relationships.

School to the community: The community provides funds to construct and maintain schools. Except in rare cases, the pupils as direct beneficiaries do not pay for their own education. Therefore, the community expects pupils to use school facilities and educational materials properly and carefully. They expect pupils to show their appreciation for their education by making maximum use of the opportunities given them. The community expects teachers to develop this sense of appreciation in students.

Pupils and staff: Adults are in the minority in most schools, but this minority is charged with the responsibility of establishing and executing the program for the entire group. The staff serves as society's representative in the school. Therefore, pupils should show respect to the staff, and the staff should show themselves worthy of this respect. The office of teacher or principal or nurse or custodian is an important one or it would not exist. Pupils should treat the office and the person charged with it with respect, and teachers have an obligation to insist on it. The staff should also realize that their positions exist because of the pupils. They are society's servants charged with serving the needs of the pupils in their particular school. Those who seek respect must also be willing to give it.

Among pupils: Immature people are usually egocentric. Most pupils are immature. The major general objective teachers should develop in the area of pupil-to-pupil relationships is honest respect for the dignity and integrity of fellow pupils, a recognition of the rights and desires of others. This means that pupils should learn to stand in line, to share facilities and equipment, to share in clean-up tasks, and to cooperate in many other ways.

Without the gradual development of the three general objectives summarized above, working conditions in schools would become intolerable in the higher grades as pupils become more assertive. But how does a teacher implement such a set of general objectives? By working at them.

And the time to begin is before school begins. During this period write specific statements that describe what you would like to develop in your pupils during the year. For example, a second grade teacher might see her task with respect to the development of respect of pupils for each other as follows:

> Pupils will show their respect for fellow pupils through commonly accepted social conventions. They will be willing to wait their turns by properly standing in line. They will use such phrases as please and thank you when working together. On their own initiative they will share things when this is necessary. . . .

A sixth grade teacher might see the situation in his room this way:

> Pupils will not abuse their position as the oldest pupils in the school. Rather, they will set a good example for younger pupils to emulate. They will be careful to obey school regulations such as walking in the hall, staying within the playgrounds, etc. They will refrain from loud and boisterous behavior during school hours. They will show their maturity in their dress and bearing. They will assist younger pupils in difficulty. . . .

You will note that these objectives aren't comprehensive. They are descriptive of behavior goals that seem important to specific teachers, and they are written in terms of realistic goals that can be reached. Remember, you don't bear the entire burden of civilizing your class.

One problem with objectives such as these is that teachers sometimes mistake observed behavior for a complete change in attitude. We can't infer that just because a second grade pupil doesn't shove in line any more, that he now respects his fellow man. On the other hand, we can question whether he respects his fellow man if he persists in shoving whenever he is in a line.

Set human relations goals for yourself and for your class. Base your goals on an honest assessment of your teaching situation. State them clearly so that you have no doubt about what you mean. Revise them during the year if necessary, but teach in terms of goals you can understand and attain. It's optimistic to expect that objectives such as those above would be attained perfectly. But it's unfair to society to make only half-hearted effort.

PREPARE THE CLASSROOM

It took me seven years to discover there was more than one way to prepare a classroom for the first day of school. I had moved to a new school and had spent Labor Day afternoon putting up exhibits and displays as was my usual custom. When I was done I stepped into the next room to see what the other sixth grade teacher had done. His room was bare, devoid of any decoration. I was shocked—what a cold way to start the year!

After school the next day I stepped into his room again. Imagine my surprise when I saw his room gaily decorated with bulletin board exhibits and pupil constructed models and displays. It looked very attractive.

On registration day he had asked pupils assigned to his room to bring along anything interesting they had made during the summer, pictures and souvenirs from trips, and anything else that classmates might like to see. First order of business the first day he assigned desks and books. Then the class set to work singly and in groups to decorate their room. Wall and shelf and bulletin board areas were parceled out. When the displays were all done the pupils returned to their desks and admired their handiwork. Each explained what he had done. And so the year began. It was a good idea, well executed.

Most teachers, however, do some preliminary decorating before the pupils arrive. Ideally such decoration should be a sampler of what pupils can expect during their year together.

The subject matter objectives of the school year can be reduced to relatively simple statements with a little effort. Visualize these basic statements with attractive displays. This will accomplish two things. It will force you to think through and simplify your teaching objectives for the year, and it will outline the year's work for your pupils the first day. You might consider developing some of your displays around questions and riddles. How can you multiply two numbers and get a product that is smaller than either number? A question like this could introduce a sixth grade class to the work they will do with fractions during the year. A bulletin board display composed of six carefully selected pictures could introduce a class to the major generalization developed in the six science units to be developed during the year.

The Language Arts program will occupy much school time during the year. Introduce pupils to the major characters they will meet in their reading books. Display a list of some of the words they will be able to spell by June. Illustrate your major goals in oral and written expression. Duplicate a puzzle or riddle page that includes a sampler of many of the language activities pupils will engage in during the year.

Don't slight the area of human relations. Develop imaginative and provocative displays that accent the specific objectives you framed for your class. For example, a teacher who wanted to develop an awareness and appreciation of the community's investment in education could set up a display that presented the value of the school plant, annual operation costs, per pupil expenditures, etc. with the caption, What Can We Give Our Community In Return? A teacher who wanted to develop respect for staff members could set up a chart that indicated the many different kinds of effort required to keep a school functioning properly. The second grade teacher mentioned above who was concerned about teaching pupils correct social conventions could find many imaginative and amusing ideas for a display in Sesyle Joslin's *What Do You Say Dear?* (Scott, 1958). The sixth grade teacher who was concerned about the example his pupils would set for younger pupils might develop a bulletin board display under the caption What Does It *Really* Mean To Be At The Top? Displays such as these are especially valuable because they can be referred to again and again during the early days of the school year.

Pre-school decorating should also explore and illustrate decorating possibilities and limitations of the classroom. Hanging things from the ceiling in a way acceptable to the administration will illustrate correct procedure without a lot of verbal explanation. So will an exhibit showing how pictures and papers can be affixed properly to a variety of wall surfaces. Display the various colors of construction paper available, samples from your picture file, and other materials pupils might consider using in later displays. Illustrate several ways of lettering.

Introduce your class to each textbook they will use through an attractive display. This is so much more pleasant than merely passing out a pile of dusty books. Include questions about the book being displayed. What can we tell about the book from the illustrations? Will the book be difficult to read? Does the author seem excited about this subject? Let pupils browse through the books. Discuss their answers to the questions when the books are distributed.

It's surprising how much four walls can do to set the tone for a year. Two approaches have been outlined. Let's examine both in terms of what they do to start a good class relationship.

The teacher who goes to extra effort to make the room look pleasing at first glance indicates his willingness to work to make the year a pleasant one. He shows that he is interested in attractive surroundings. By developing imaginative and challenging displays around the tasks at hand rather than around innocuous displays of fall flowers, he shows an enthusiasm for learning and teaching. Enthusiasm is contagious. His efforts are usually rewarded. Teachers who work to sell learning to their pupils from the pupils' first glance into the classroom are convinced it is well worth the effort to prepare a classroom attractively. They continue to do it every September. And they surprise and delight their own children with a beautifully decorated Christmas tree one morning four months later.

The teacher who resists the temptation to make the room "only his" by covering all available wall space before the pupils have a chance to contribute their ideas shows pupils he understands their wish to be involved in decorating their classroom. By scheduling time from the very first day, and by having plenty of materials available for decorating, he shows that the walls aren't bare because he was too lazy to decorate them. He is sure enough of his position and ability to know that his success or failure with his class doesn't rest on their first glance into the room. And he involves his whole family in Christmas tree decorating four months later.

Two forms of love for a class—one reveals itself in expression, the other in repression. Which is better? It would seem that either approach could help establish a good class relationship if the reason for the approach is clearly communicated at first meeting. It's not so much what you do, but that you communicate a deep love and concern for the sensitivities of your class through the procedures you follow.

2

BEGIN THE YEAR
EFFECTIVELY

MAKE A GOOD FIRST IMPRESSION

Even teachers who habitually arrive as late as regulations allow arrive early the first day of school. They usually bring along some stomach butterflies too. Few teachers are completely nonchalant about meeting their new charges for the first time. There is usually at least a bit of nervous expectation. It shows itself in a little extra effort during the morning shaving or make-up routine, in the selection of the best outfit to wear, in a morning newspaper read with the mind already at school, in an extra look in the mirror before leaving. All this because teachers are concerned about a good first impression.

What sort of impression should a teacher attempt to give the first day? Good guy? Benevolent despot? Intellectual leader? The Boss? Friend of the downtrodden and distressed? Efficiency expert? Pal? Keeper of the torture house for miscreants? Man of the world? Suzy Sophisticate? Drudge? Top teacher (you're-lucky-to-be-in-my-room)? Mr. Chipps? Socrates? Miss Dove?

Just you! With 180 days to go, don't try to put on an act. Be yourself. There must be something personable and redeemable about you or you wouldn't have been hired. Show that. Maybe that places you in one of the categories above—so be it. But don't try to pass yourself off the first day as someone you're not. You can't keep up the act indefinitely if you're new; if you've been around for awhile, it won't do any good because your reputation has preceded you. Make the best of yourself, whatever that is. That's the best you can do the first day. A person who is acting naturally is usually as relaxed as he ever gets. And people rarely make a good impression when they are tense.

Forget about what you're *not* going to do or allow. Concentrate on what you're going to do or allow. It's the difference between telling pupils they can't leave their seats and asking them to remain in their seats. By approaching your class in a positive manner, you accomplish as much, and you show yourself in a better light. Your class hopes you will be a good teacher. It will be a long year if you're not. So try to set them at ease the first day by making a good impression.

Concentrate on five traits students commonly list when they are asked to indicate what traits a teacher should have: competence, genuine warmth, a sense of humor, orderliness, and good grooming. Your class will want to know about these right off.

Competence: Nobody wants to do business with a second-rate brain surgeon—or with a second-rate teacher. Don't pretend you are more competent than you are—you'll get caught in that web in a few days. But don't show yourself less competent than you are, either. That's just as senseless. It's really not difficult to show a sufficient level of competency for the first day. Be thoroughly familiar with school policies and regulations. Be efficient and businesslike as you lead your charges through the day. And teach the type of lessons all intelligent teachers teach on opening days, principal's visits, and other festive occasions. In other words, plan the day carefully. Set a high teaching standard the first day. It will impress your class, but more important, it will give you something good to shoot at the second day.

Genuine warmth: Greet pupils warmly as they come into your room. Show them you're happy they came. Be big enough to do things for them. One teacher who is widely respected for his distinguished bearing, his wide grasp of his field, and his teaching ability, typically helps his students with their coats, scurries around to bring in extra chairs when needed, always has a supply of sharpened pencils to trade for dull ones, and in other ways sees to it that his class is comfortable and prepared for his instruction. "He reminds a guy of Jesus washing

His disciples' feet." That student's comparison is apt. [Good teachers are characterized by their willingness to do whatever work is required to make the class period a worthwhile experience. Nothing is too menial for them in their pursuit of this goal. They consider their students very important people.]

It would seem that this expression of genuine warmth would be particularly applicable in schools where many pupils come from poor home situations, where they have to be on their own too much of the time, where they have learned to mistrust adults. These students have a special need to know that we are happy to have them in our classrooms, that we exist as a profession for *them*.

A sense of humor: If ever a profession needed a sense of humor to keep it going, it is the teaching profession. Our work does not bring immediate or dramatic results as a lawyer's, surgeon's, carpenter's or fireman's work does. It takes a sense of humor to keep at it when each day's work is such a short step forward. Perhaps this is why pupils rate a sense of humor so high in their lists of desirable traits in teachers. They too sense the frustration in teaching.

It's really not difficult to show your class the first day that you have a sense of humor, if you have one. Anyone can smile. That's not much, but it's a start. More important—don't take yourself too seriously. Select something that's funny about you, whether it's your name, your size, your shape, your hair or lack of it, or whatever it is. Joke about it. A class is always happy to hear that their teacher can laugh at himself; and having discovered that, they usually stop making jokes about him. A sense of humor involves more than a good joke or two the first day, but that much is a good starter.

A sense of orderliness: Most pupils prefer an orderly atmosphere in school, even though they may do little to promote it themselves. Establish orderly procedures the first day. Arrive at school early enough to complete all office and other out-of-classroom activities before pupils arrive. Don't leave the room between the time pupils arrive and the time school starts. Ask pupils to be seated when they arrive, and give them something to do: a form to fill out, some questions to answer. Keep them occupied. Arrange desks in some traditional manner, or use the arrangement their last teacher used. You will have 179 days to introduce variations in their school life. Play the first day conservatively.

Good grooming: We often forget that our students spend much of their time looking at us. A teacher looks at thirty pupils, but thirty pupils look at one teacher. Perhaps good grooming doesn't mean much one way or another to any of our pupils, but some pupils in every class do notice last year's styles, ill-fitting clothes, unkempt hair, poor color combinations, and the like. It's not too much to dress up a little for pupils if we force them to look at us constantly. An adult teacher should dress and act as a person with polish.

A good first impression is important, but it will only get you through the first day or the first few days, unless that impression accurately describes the sort of person you are, and unless that person is worth knowing better.

INTRODUCE WITH A FLAIR

The first day of school can be a lonely one for new pupils. Generally, many pupils in the class were classmates the year before, or at least are acquainted with each other. New pupils feel left out. They are lonesome for their old school and classmates. One of the first tasks facing a teacher is to help these pupils overcome their feelings of shyness and loneliness, to get them acquainted with their new classmates and to weld the entire group of old and new pupils into a class.

Do this with a flair. Don't give the old-timers a chance to stand off with each other. Get them involved in greeting the new pupils. Don't give the new pupils a chance to stand off and feel lonesome. Get them involved in meeting new friends. Games can be used to good advantage. A few minutes spent in such activity will pay big dividends. Such introductory activities should accomplish three things: Get names straight, give background information, and break the ice. The activities suggested below will help you welcome new pupils to your school and develop a group spirit in your class.

Get the names straight: Meet the first pupil at the door with a tape recorder. Introduce yourself and welcome him to your room, recording the greeting. Show him how to work the tape recorder and ask him to welcome and introduce the next pupil who arrives. Ask each succeeding pupil to welcome the next pupil until all have arrived. Don't forget to add your own personal greeting after each little taping session is completed. Play the tape when school begins. Ask pupils to stand while the recording of their introduction is played. A side benefit of this activity is that pupils learn how to operate the tape recorder.

When all pupils have been seated, find out who would be first in an alphabetical listing. Ask him to start a receiving line in front of the room. As you work out the alphabetical list with the class, ask each succeeding person to go down the line and shake hands with those who preceded him. Enter the pupils' names in your record book before they sit down. It's a lot pleasanter developing an alphabetical listing this way than by shuffling entrance forms.

Ask each pupil to identify his desk with a name card. Encourage pupils to develop folded cards with their names written on several sides so the cards can be read from different parts of the room.

At the end of the first day, pin a number from 1 to 10 on each pupil. Call out a larger number such as 34. Pupils quickly assemble in groups until their numbers total the number called. Leftovers form a group of their own. Point to a person in each group. He must immediately identify every other person in his group.

At the end of the day for several days spend a minute or two calling out initials of pupils. The pupil whose initials were called rises immediately. The class calls out his name. Or the last person to rise calls out the name.

Give background information: Develop a duplicated list of questions based on information available in pupils' folders. Ask the class to write the name of the pupils who matches the items. Sample questions might include: Which three boys have the same middle name? Whose birthday is on December 25? Whose father is a baker? Each pupil should be represented with an item. Set aside 15 minutes for this activity or ask pupils to work at it at odd moments during the first day.

Play "Dividing up the Room." Push the desks aside and divide the room into 12 zones, or use the gym or an outdoor area. Develop a list of statements such as: Everyone whose family name ends with T go to zone 8; everyone whose family name ends with M go to zone 5; with Y to zone 10; with R to zone 7: all the rest go to zone 1. Or, Go to the zone number that is the same as the number of children in your family. Or, Go to the zone number that is the same as the number of letters in your last name. Ask each pupil to keep track of the zone numbers he entered. The pupils with the highest and lowest totals win.

Give each pupil a sheet of paper with a vertical list of as many numbers as there are pupils. Ask pupils to pair signatures as on a dance card. At odd moments during the first few days call out one of the numbers. The pupils pair off. Give them a conversation category such as favorite foods, hobbies, most exciting adventure, etc. Ask the couples to discuss the subject for a stipulated time of two or three minutes.

Many teachers ask pupils to recount their summer experiences some time during the first day or two. This gets rather dreary after the twentieth tale has been told. One interesting variation is to ask pupils to write their stories without signing their names. Collect the papers, shuffle them, and pass them out at random. After each pupil reads the paper he received, the class tries to guess the author. Or number the papers and pin them to the bulletin board. See who can identify the most correctly. The same activity can be carried out with a tape recorder. It's interesting to try to identify voices.

"Break the ice": Use the Big Brother and Big Sister approach to help new pupils. Assign each new pupil to one who attended the school last year. Ask the old pupils to help the newcomers get acquainted.

Do a few silly things. Use a ruler to measure the widest grin, a thermometer to measure the warmest handshake. Or have a humming championship. Pair the class off. At your signal each pupil looks his partner in the eye and starts humming. First one to take a breath loses. Winners pair off again and repeat the process until the champion hummer is selected. It's all right to try to make your opponent laugh, but no tickling in the ribs.

A postscript: Don't forget to introduce yourself. Your pupils will want to know about you. Tell them about yourself and your family. Don't tell it all the first day though. Make it a continuing story that lasts as long as you work with them. Let them know you are a warm human being with loves and interests that take them all in and a wide circle besides.

MAKE THE FIRST DAY COUNT*

A class is usually unusually attentive during the first day of the school year. They're filled with anticipation. More often than not, though, they spend much of the day receiving textbooks and materials, inspecting the physical layout of the room, and listening to the teacher make a prosaic presentation of school policies and regulations. They participate in the proceedings only with their eyes and ears and seat.

With a little imagination, you can capitalize on this first day enthusiasm and involve the pupils in these presentations. It will take a little longer, but it's well worth the time and effort. The class will get more out of the experience, and you will have a fine opportunity to size up the individual and group potential of your class.

The areas listed below are commonly covered during the first day. If you involve pupils in these presentations, you will have to assemble the information they will need to prepare their presentations. Since time is a factor, concentrate on the presentation of information rather than on the gathering of information. Everything they need for a good report should be readily available.

Divide the class into groups. Assign one of the topics below to each group. You might also want to suggest the medium they will use to present their report, particularly if you want to demonstrate the variety of procedures they might consider in future committee reports. For example, if you have a small puppet stage, ask one of the groups to use puppets in presenting its report. Another group might report via tape recorder, another via bulletin board, another through a panel discussion. Agree on work procedures, and give the groups time to study their assignments and prepare their reports. Move about as they do their work and assist in any way possible. Anticipate requests for materials so you won't have to leave the room during the period. Study the group interaction. Do all participate? Do a few try to dominate? How much tendency towards horseplay is evident? When all groups

---

* Parts of this section and the next were first published as an article titled, "Only 179 Days To Go," INSTRUCTOR, September, 1962, p. 33ff.

are ready, ask them to present their reports. Supplement the reports when necessary, and spend some time discussing issues raised by the presentations.

School policies: Provide the committee with a statement of various school policies you want presented to the class. Encourage them to think of an imaginative way of presenting these to the class. Perhaps they could use a tape recorder to interview the principal, secretary, custodian, nurse, and cook on various aspects of school policies. Perhaps they could incorporate these policies into an imaginative bulletin board display that could be left up for several weeks. Perhaps they could work out a quiz game on the policies and then concentrate class discussion on the items the pupils missed.

Fire and safety: Provide the committee with policies, procedures, and suggestions. They should lead the class through a fire drill. They could demonstrate procedures that should be followed when accidents occur at school. They could investigate and report on any dangerous areas in the school and playground and propose procedures for students in these areas. They should also report on street crossing policies and the work of the safety patrol. Perhaps they could invite a patrol boy to address the class.

The classroom: Encourage this committee to make a thorough examination of the classroom. They ought to report on where and how things can be affixed to the walls. They should suggest policies for storing things so that the room can be kept as neat as possible. They should consider how the class can make the custodian's work easier. They could study and report on traffic flow with various desk arrangements. They ought to point out areas where the floor gets slippery when wet, where the sun glares, where heat comes into the room. If time allows they could lead the class into an exploration of the various surface areas in the room, such as walls, desks, floor, books, gratings, and window frames. Ask the pupils to make crayon rubbings of these surfaces. These can be cut out and pasted into collage designs. Most pupils are surprised at the variety of surface areas found in a classroom.

Reference measures: Weights and measures will be mentioned frequently during the year. A textbook will report that something is 500 feet long. A class discussion will bring out something in the news that weighs 30 pounds. Assign a committee to weigh and measure various things, the area of the floor, the height of the room, the weight of various textbooks, the distance to the office, etc. Ask them to make a chart showing selected findings. Later, when they read that something is 500 feet long, they will know that's twice the length of the school; when they hear that something weighs 30 pounds, they can assemble and lift a pile of 15 arithmetic books.

Textbooks and materials: Ask this committee to organize and record the distribution of texts and materials. In addition, ask them to prepare and present a puppet play or skit on book care. They might also demonstrate several ways to make book jackets. A trip to the school library and a report on library policies might also be arranged.

Spend the rest of the first day introducing the class to the subjects they will study during the year. Some suggestions for wall displays were given in Chapter 1. While you will have to be responsible for most of this, you can also involve pupils in this preview if you set your imagination to it.

One interesting way to involve pupils in this preview of the subjects they will study during the year is to play a variation on the popular TV game, *College Quiz Bowl*. Select teams of boys and girls or play all the boys against all the girls. Develop an interesting list of questions from the texts and materials they will use during the year. Select questions that will give the class an overview of the year. Sample items might include: How do you spell *separate*? What is the square root of 25? What is the capital of Greece? How many members does the U.S. Senate have? Name a local bird that doesn't migrate. What is the area of a circle with a diameter of 14 inches? Pupils can signal by slapping their hands on their desks. This game will give you a good indication of how much pupils already know of material to be studied during the year.

Toward the end of the first day ask the class to write short essays outlining their plans and hopes for the year. Collect the papers, place them unread in a large envelope, seal it, and file it away until the last day of the school year. Open the envelope then and return the papers. It's always interesting to read in June what you wrote last September. You might ask pupils to turn their papers over and write an evaluation of the year on the basis of fulfilled and unfulfilled hopes and plans. It will make interesting reading for you after you have said good-by to them for the last time.

But then, we're getting ahead of ourselves. There are still 178 days of school in between.

MAKE THE FIRST WEEK COUNT EVEN MORE

Work and behavior patterns are generally established during the first week. Inexperienced teachers often take a wait-and-see attitude. They wait to see how things will shape up before deciding how they will handle the class during the year. By then it's often too late. Experienced teachers usually operate on the theory that it's better to get down to business right away and shake the summer sun out of the class. They keep the class busy all week with activities that require heavy pupil involvement and allow plenty of opportunities to size up the group. They know it's easier to ease up the second week than it is to tighten up.

Teachers often concentrate on written assignments the first week. These give the teacher a good opportunity to study pupils at work. It's much easier to observe and work with problem pupils individually if the rest of the class is occupied with work they can carry out alone. Shy pupils who would ordinarily not participate in class discussions the first few weeks will participate with less reluctance (and often with enthusiasm) in written activities. Written assignments also give teachers the opportunity to analyze pupil responses in the contemplative hours after school.

This is not to imply that pupils should spend their first week working their way through several hundred long-division problems. That's busy work—a poor way to start the year. Rather, seek the imaginative touch in written work you assign. Select written assignments with particular care. Select activities that are well-suited to written treatment, and that are worth the time and effort spent on them. Then add an imaginative twist that will also impress a point in classroom living. Some examples?

Instead of asking the class to actually do an assignment, duplicate a typical completed paper that might be handed in by a pupil. As you construct this paper, include a good sampling of normal pupil errors. Distribute a copy of the paper to each pupil. Ask pupils to correct and grade the paper using the grading system employed in the school. Tabulate their grades on the board. In most cases you will discover much variation in the grades given by pupils. Discuss this and your own evaluation and grading procedures with the class using the duplicated paper and their grades as a frame of reference.

"Read the chapter and answer the questions at the end." This rather common and uninspiring assignment can be made more interesting and more valuable with imaginative touches. If you want to acquaint your class with reference works available to them, ask them to read the chapter and then seek out one fact about the material covered that was not included in the text. Share findings and discuss textbook limitations. Compare the reference works used by the pupils.

If you want to discuss differences that exist among people ask your class to ask questions on the chapter instead of answering them. Ask one pupil to ask questions on the chapter that a musician might ask, another questions a soldier might ask, another questions a scientist might ask, another questions a businessman might ask, etc. Read their questions to the class. Note with them how different people viewed the same set of data differently. Continue with a class discussion on differences of background and interest found in the class.

Many pupils read instructions carelessly. Use this activity to begin a class discussion on the importance of following instructions. Hand out a duplicated sheet with these items on it. Allow only four minutes for completion.

CAN YOU FOLLOW DIRECTIONS?

(Complete in 4 minutes) _____

1. Read everything before doing anything.
2. Print your name on the line in the upper right hand corner.
3. Underline the word *Print* in sentence two.
4. Draw five small circles to the right of this sentence.
5. Put an X in each circle.
6. Enclose all five circles in a rectangle.
7. Underline the word *anything* in sentence one.

8. Draw a circle around each word in sentence seven.
9. On the reverse side of this paper, multiply 12345679 x 45.
10. Draw a small square in the lower left hand corner of this paper.
11. Draw a circle inside the square.
12. Your answer in number nine should be nine fives. Write five nines after this sentence.
13. If you think you have followed all directions up to this point, print the word YES after this sentence.
14. Say the six times multiplication table aloud in your normal speaking voice.
15. Write your teacher's name in front of this sentence.
16. Draw a triangle below the number 13 above.
17. Print the word YES behind the title of this paper.
18. Call out your first name so that your teacher can hear it.
19. Underline all of sentence one.
20. Now that you have finished reading everything as requested in sentence one, do only what is asked in sentence two. Ignore the other 18 items. Sit back and listen to those who didn't read sentence one call out the six times tables and their names.

What can a teacher do to make those long-division problems interesting? Assign a page of problems. When the class is finished, write the answers on the board and ask the pupils to correct their own papers. Then ask them to analyze their papers and discover why they made the mistakes they made. Finally ask them to write an essay describing their difficulties, if any, with long-division (or multiplication, or solid geometry, or grammar). Ask them to indicate in the paper where they need to improve and to suggest what they might do to improve their work in future assignments.

Note how the small changes suggested above add a touch of challenge to routine written assignments. Most written assignments can be improved if teachers would but put their minds to the task. It's worth the effort if it gets the year off to a better start.

The first week of school is more than written assignments. Tentative groupings should be made. Pupils should get an overview of the things that will be studied. The thirty some individuals should be welded into a group. Classroom standards and rules will have to be developed. All the more reason for an imaginatively planned, well-organized first week.

AGREE ON GROUND RULES

Most teachers want to be consulted when faculty and school policies are determined. They resent it when policies are handed down from Olympus before they have a chance to react to the proposals. Pupils feel the same way about classroom procedures and policies.

Fearful administrators and fearful teachers worry that those under them will propose and adopt ridiculous and unworkable policies if they are given the opportunity. This is nonsense. It shows a lack of understanding of the way people act. It supposes that only a select few have the wisdom to understand the requirements of group living. Granted, there are exceptions. It might be folly for a Reform School teacher to grant exceptional advisory and assentive powers to his class. But how many of us teach in such a situation?

Pupils come to school with a set of expectations about school life that are well-grounded in the community where they live. At home they have lived with adult authority figures. Many of them have shared a room with others of approximately the same age. They have played with neighborhood children. They have come to know freedom and restriction. They know each has bounds. Is school life such a departure from community life?

The longer a pupil is in school the more his knowledge of school culture is increased. His knowledge and experience isn't as complete as his teacher's, but it's worth serious consideration. He has lived in the same type of classroom environment as his teacher. He knows that thirty people can leave a room much more easily if they walk than if they form a stampede. He knows excessive noise is distracting. He knows society expects him to expend some effort at learning. He doesn't always act on the basis of his knowledge, but then, isn't that a goal of education—to turn knowledge into action?

Classroom procedures and policies should be determined early in the school year. And pupils should be involved in some of the deliberations and decisions. They may be immature and inconsistent in their approach to the problem. They may make wrong decisions. But they're more apt to work with you than against you if they sense that they were treated honestly in their participation, that a class consensus of sorts was reached, that a reasonable decision was achieved, and that they made a commitment regarding their future behavior. That's the best way to turn knowledge into action.

Be honest with them: Prepare your presentation and discussion of class behavior standards and rules carefully. Pupils can detect attempts to manipulate them. They resent pious protestations of democratic decisions when the discussion is structured so that the final decision is obvious from the beginning. They resent it with the same intensity that teachers resent such action from administrators.

Begin by establishing boundaries. Some behavior areas are out of the jurisdiction of pupils because they involve administrative responsibility, other classes, or established schedules. Cafeteria and playground schedules and procedures might be in this category. Some activities are the prerogative or responsibility of the teacher; for example, procedures for handing in written work, or the arrangement of desks. Some areas rightfully involve pupils; for example, the operation of a class organization, the sharing of limited playground equipment during recess, behavior during study periods. Clearly outline areas of responsibility to the class, however these are defined in your school. Let pupils know where they have no responsibility (and why), where they can serve in an advisory capacity, and where they have decision making responsibility. And then keep discussion and decision within these boundaries.

Reach real consensus: Research studies have indicated that group consensus is important if group decisions are to be implemented. Consensus is not necessarily the same as decision. Pupils will often vote for something, not because they are really in favor of it, but because they like or fear the teacher. Guiding a class discussion towards a positive consensus requires much skill on the part of the teacher.

Allow plenty of time for the discussion so pupils won't feel they are being pressured toward an immediate decision. If necessary, continue the discussion the next day if no consensus is reached. Encourage participation from all pupils. Ask them to write suggestions on paper, and then list these on the board if it appears that some children will not participate orally, or that those who do participate the most frequently do not speak for the class.

Reflect and deflect responses when necessary. Children will often say things in class discussion that appear to have little relationship with the discussion at hand. If you can discover a relationship, restate what has been said in terms that indicate the relationship. Such reflection, if honestly done, will encourage participation from pupils who are unable to phrase their thoughts clearly. Deflection means that the contribution is rephrased in question form and turned back to the group. This very effective technique helps move the discussion towards solution. For example, if a girl would say, "I don't think it's fair to let the boys have the soccer ball three days a week even if there are more boys," the teacher might re-phrase her contribution, "Why would it or why wouldn't it be fair to let the boys have the soccer ball three days a week?"

Don't let your biases show through your voice and manner in such a discussion. Be available to give needed information, to serve as moderator, and to steer the discussion towards an acceptable solution. Remember, these problems are primarily theirs. You *will* reduce later difficulties if you do all in your power to reach a real consensus of pupil opinion on issues where their advice and consent is sought. Group pressure will be on your side with consensus. Without it, it's you against them.

Be patient with indecision and wrong decision: Suppose the class can't decide who should have the soccer ball three days a week. A good solution might be quite obvious to you but not to them. Often, pupil groups lack the intelligence and/or maturity to make decisions that are fairly obvious to adults. At times like that it's good to remember that if pupils knew as much as adults, they wouldn't be going to school. It may take a class longer to come to a decision without your advice, but sometimes it's worth the extra time and effort. And then there are times when it is foolish to have a mature adult in the room and not make use of his wider knowledge and experience. There is no formula for correct action in this matter except to come into the discussion when you must and stay out whenever you can.

Try to arrive at an agreement on ground rules during the first week. Differentiate between standards of behavior which are primarily agreements among class members on how they will behave when their behavior affects only themselves, and school rules which deal with behavior that affects others. These are teacher or school imposed, and not necessarily subject to student ratification. If teacher and pupils understand the function of each, things should go smoother during the year.

Will all pupils act perfectly all year? Hardly. But they may act better, and it's always good to begin the year on an optimistic note.

SMOOTH THE WAY FOR LATE ENROLLEES

School starts late for many pupils. They arrive as the last leaf is falling, while the snow is swirling, even with the daffodils. In this mobile age children change schools during the entire school year. Most children are unhappy over the move. Even a father's promotion and transfer mean little compared to the loss of neighborhood friends. The move occupies the time and energy of parents, and the children are left to fend for themselves much of the time in a new environment.

Few teachers can hope to go through the year without adding at least one pupil. Most pupils adapt to their new school with surprising ease. But two types of pupils have difficulty. The shy pupil who needed a long time to work up the small circle of friends he had in his former school sees the prospect of starting fresh in the middle of the year as a frightening task. And the pupil who continues to live in spirit in his former school, and who dotes on how much better things were back there makes a pest of himself in time.

The easiest way to deal with late enrollees is to plan for them early in the school year, before they show up. Bring up the subject the first week or so, while many of the pupils in the class are still in similar circumstances, getting acquainted in a new school. They will be much more sympathetic with the problem then. You might begin by asking the class how many had enrolled in a school after the school year had begun. Ask them to relate their experiences, particularly the problems they faced. Ask for suggestions to smooth the way for any late enrollees who might come. Develop a plan of action through the discussion and carry it out when new pupils come.

This is a good project for a class organization. They might elect a welcoming committee that would have this as one of its responsibilities.

New pupils should be involved in school routine and activities without calling undue attention to them. Different pupils could serve as hosts during each day of the first week and simply involve the new pupil in their normal activities. Most pupils are able to take care of themselves after a week or so.

Place new pupils' names on any room lists (monitor, plant watering, etc.) immediately. Construct such lists so names can be added easily. I can recall one child telling me that she had felt left out for a long time because her name was written on a slip of white paper I had handy and pasted to the master sheet, while the other pupils who had been in the room from the first had their names written on yellow paper. A childish attitude? Yes, but then she was a child.

Spend some time with new pupils the first several days. The after school hours are often good for this. Chat with them informally. Ask about their former friends and school. You won't learn much while you're talking so let them do most of the talking and you do most of the listening. Discuss differences between the two schools, and point out why things are sometimes done differently in different schools. Be sympathetic, but also be positive about their move.

Pupils who have difficulty adjusting to a move require extra care over a longer period. There is no magic formula for dealing with these pupils. They do usually require large doses of love and patience. Don't neglect to meet with their parents. Such pupils usually bring home tales of unhappy experiences at school and these accent any home and family problems arising from a move. Don't neglect to get them involved in school activities. Homesickness tends to diminish as a person gets involved in activities in his new home.

POSTSCRIPT

And so the year begins. August and September are busy times for a teacher. They determine much of what happens during succeeding months. Careful attention paid to seemingly insignificant details during these months can pay big dividends later. So much of what teachers do these months has an emotional impact on students. We attempt to develop individual sensitivity through a mass individualized educational agency. It is important, therefore, that teachers begin the year with a healthy concern for the sensitivities of the individual rather than an eagerness to get to the institutionalized and conformist side of formal education. This necessity to make haste slowly at the beginning of the year will make many special demands on you. Other teachers have worked it out, though, and so can you.

PART II:
DURING THE DAYS AND WEEKS
AND MONTHS

3

DEVELOP GOOD
DAILY ROUTINE

USE ROUTINE PROPERLY

There comes a day when beginnings are over and the year is under way. Beginnings are important, but most of the real work of the school year is accomplished when minor and recurring decisions don't have to be decided anew every day, when pupils know what comes after arithmetic and get ready without reminding, when room monitors can take lunch count in two minutes instead of ten, when pupils know how to title, identify, and turn in written work without being told.

Firmly established routines are an integral part of a smoothly functioning classroom. They free you and your class for more important activities than deciding every day who will feed the goldfish. They reduce arguments among pupils over procedures and turns. They teach pupils to budget their time wisely. And over the years they develop a pecking order of sorts in pupils' minds over the relative importance of activities and decisions that can and should be reduced to routine, and those that should not be reduced to routine.

I can recall being taken to task once for not letting my class begin the day by deciding the order of the day's activities. While a brief preview and discussion of the day's activities has some merit, it's sheer nonsense to spend the first twenty minutes or so of a busy school day juggling the order of the schedule in the name of democracy. There are enough significant issues to discuss and decide with a class at the beginning of the school day without rehashing something that can just as well stay relatively constant for days on end. By always placing such minor decisions above the level of routine, you make them more important in the minds of pupils than they should be. Such pupils grow up to serve as chairmen of organizations that spend so much of their meeting time arguing minor procedural points that they don't get around to important issues that need discussion until everyone is argued out and eager for adjournment.

There will be times when normally routine activities, such as the sequence of the day's schedule, should be removed from the level of routine, discussed, and temporarily changed. No routine procedure is sensible and efficient all the time. We still have to decide when to follow established routines and when to vary from them. This freedom to question and vary routine procedures, though not frequently used, keeps life with regulations and restrictions from becoming unbearable, because it makes the individual more important than the routine.

What should be reduced to the level of routine? Practice will vary in schools and classrooms, but many teachers normally reduce the following activities to some form of routine.

Procedures for:

> Transactions with the school office, library, and nurse
> Eating in the cafeteria
> Leaving the room during fire drills and for assembly and dismissal at other times when school bells ring
> Entering and leaving classrooms and for walking along corridors
> Making clothing changes, such as for PE, art, recess, and going home
> Regulating inside the classroom traffic, such as getting and distributing books and supplies, sharpening pencils, and getting drinks
> Going to the restroom
> Titling, identifying, and turning in written work
> Conducting room elections and making class decisions
> Housekeeping chores carried on in the classroom
> Greeting classroom visitors

As much as possible develop classroom routines with the advice and consent of the pupils. Routine procedures developed with the consensus of the class will work much more effectively than procedures prescribed by you without their consultation. You might use one of the following approaches to enlist the cooperation of your class.

When the year is sufficiently under way, discuss the normal daily activities with your class in the context of establishing which activities might be classified as routine and which non-routine. Through class discussion work out procedures for dealing efficiently with each type of activity.

List possible routine activities on a duplicated sheet of paper. Ask each pupil to write suggested procedures that might be followed in dealing with each activity. Select a class committee to tabulate and report on the suggestions given. Adopt proposed routines where there is general agreement. Discuss others until a consensus is reached. In cases where no consensus is reached, consider the activity non-routine and deal with it each time it comes up.

Review routine procedures periodically. Select a committee to review procedures in the light of class behavior. They might propose modifications that can be considered in a class discussion on the subject. A class may have agreed at the beginning of the year that they didn't need to be dismissed row by row at recess time and that they could leave informally without incident. If they demonstrate that they can, let them continue to dismiss informally. There is no need for a formal routine dismissal procedure in that room. If, however, they demonstrate an inability to leave informally without incident, then they will have to discuss the matter anew and possibly place restraints on themselves. Democratic action implies responsible action. Only through such a program of constant evaluation will pupils discover that routine procedures are merely conventions people adopt to live more easily with each other. They have no purpose beyond that.

While accidents and illness do not occur on schedule, establish routines your class can use when such things occur. If you are not in the immediate vicinity, pupils should inform you immediately. The sick or injured pupil should remain where he is until someone competent to judge the situation has arrived. If the report sounds serious, send the pupil reporting on to the school nurse or office while you hasten to the scene. The importance of keeping your composure can't be over-emphasized. A nervous teacher at the scene of an accident can make the situation much worse. If you don't know how to administer first-aid in accidents likely to occur at school, register for a first-aid course in your community. A child's life could hang in the balance. Inform parents if medical treatment seems necessary. Unless they can't be reached, they should make such decisions. Be thoroughly familiar with all school policies dealing with sickness and accidents. You won't have time to look them up when something occurs.

Some school activities should never be reduced to the level of routine. Overemphasis on one teaching approach can make teaching routine. The history of education reports the rise and decline of several teaching approaches that were hailed as imaginative, effective, and efficient in their time but bogged down as they became routine. The Lancastrian Method and the Herbartian Method are two such examples. But don't be too quick to point the finger of scorn at our forefathers. Check your own lesson plans first. Do they have a sameness about them that smacks of formula teaching? Even teachers who do a lot of unit teaching must constantly watch that their units don't become bogged down in routine procedures and lose the spark they should have.

Activities carried on by the class in which opinions and approaches can and should vary depending on the circumstances should not be reduced to routine, if at all possible. For example, classroom parties sometimes become reduced to a set pattern or routine. Pupils play three games and then have punch and cookies. There is something to be said for traditions, but it's questionable if class parties should be placed in that category. The existence of such routine procedures for having fun certainly would have a stifling effect on whatever creative urges a committee might have. Encourage new and different approaches in such situations.

The relationship a teacher develops individually with his pupils should not become routine, or at least it should not appear routine to his pupils. Many teachers follow an admirable custom of spending some time individually with each pupil several times during the year in informal discussions. This loses much of its spontaneity if it becomes too routine; if pupils always come to the teacher's desk, if it's always carried out during a certain study period, if it's done alphabetically, and/or if it follows a set pattern.

In general, reduce activities to routine if such action improves instruction by serving the individual pupil as well as the class and school. Resist routine procedures if many people have to adjust their normal preference and behavior for the advantage and convenience of one person or a small group of people. Routine activities need not be dull and inflexible. They are an important framework that frees the imaginative teacher from detail and decisions that could sap his time and energy—frees him for greater efforts in the creative aspects of teaching. But you must take advantage of that freedom. It doesn't follow automatically.

ARRANGE SEATING TO FOSTER GROUP INTERACTION

The shape of the room and the type of desk determine seating possibilities and flexibility. Individual tables and chairs seem to offer greatest flexibility. The tables can be arranged together to form larger flat surface areas that are useful in various class projects. The unattached chairs can be arranged by themselves in more intimate circle and horseshoe discussion patterns or in theater style for classroom skits and plays. Tables and chairs double the number of pieces of furniture in the room, and this can lead to additional noise and confusion unless it is carefully controlled; but this problem does not outweigh the advantage of the flexibility of tables and chairs.

Desks with attached seats have an advantage in that the seat is usually more adapted to the posture of the pupil, something not always present in separate tables and chairs. It's questionable, however, if this posture control is such a real advantage in today's classrooms where pupils normally are not required to sit at their desks for long periods of time.

Unfastened desks and tables serve a useful purpose only if their flexibility is put to good use. Too many teachers maintain the same desk arrangement in their rooms all year long. Only the custodian benefits from furniture flexibility in those rooms. This is unfortunate because the seating arrangement can do much to affect the behavior of the pupils and the quality of the activities carried on. There are times when all pupils will want to see the teacher or someone else who is making a presentation. There are times when the pupils will want to see each other in face-to-face interaction. There are times when the class should be divided into small groups. And there are times when pupils will want to concentrate on some solitary task. Each of these situations implies a different seating arrangement. Each could occur in a single day.

Teachers are loath to arrange their schedule so that pupils must shift their desks often during the day. Each move involves noise and more time than teachers feel should be spent on such activities. What is needed is a seating arrangement that can be changed quickly and easily to meet the various circumstances indicated above.

No seating arrangement is perfect, but Figure 2 shows an arrange-

Figure 2.

ment for a class of 32 that meets most of the requirements and problems listed above. Using the typical 20″ × 24″ tables it requires a space 22′ wide and 20′ long, but this can be adjusted to meet various class and room size requirements. Note that the arrangement is nothing more than a traditional row arrangement with two of the rows staggered, and with pupils arranged in pairs. The rows can be staggered alternately, and you can use a different number of rows, but the arrangement shown here seems to work as well as any variation on it.

The paired pupils arrangement can lead to behavior problems. Usually, though, the problem centers around one or two pupils, and

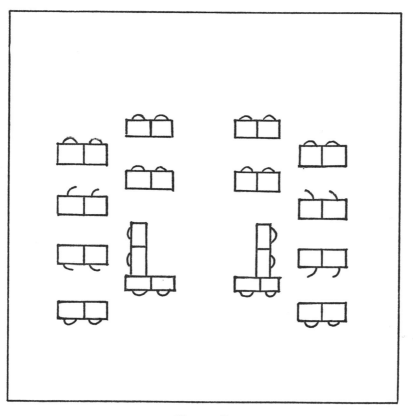

Figure 3.

they can be assigned to front corner tables with the tables separated a foot or so from their neighbors. The paired arrangement allows for greater distances overall between desks, and this is valuable for individual study. The staggered rows give a greater feeling of privacy than traditionally fixed rows. Also note how this arrangement adds a semicircle to the front of the room for presentations.

Figure 3 shows a simple move for an all class discussion in which there is maximum face-to-face interaction. It requires 12 pupils to move their chairs around to the other side of their tables, and only four pupils are required to turn their tables.

Figure 4 shows five small discussion groups. Note the horseshoe arrangement that is particularly good for promoting group discussion

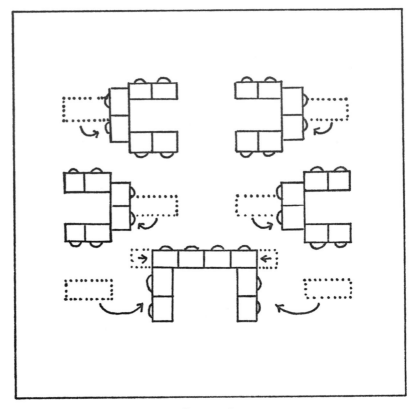

Figure 4.

and thinking. The dotted lines show that this move requires relatively little furniture shifting. The horseshoe arrangement can be easily converted to triangular arrangements that give the impression of all sitting around a large table.

Many other arrangements are possible, regardless of the shape of the room or the size of your class. Sketch a diagram of your room with all fixed walls and equipment drawn in. Make paper cut-outs to scale of all movable furniture. Move these around to discover the basic arrangement and variations that suit you and your class best. Then use it.

Schedule activities so that you can rearrange desks or tables just before a natural break such as recess, milk break, or gym period. Then the desks will be arranged properly when the class returns, and you will be able to get right to work. Pupils generally react favorably to such temporary changes in arrangement.

Change the seating arrangement frequently. Give the pupils a chance to sit near many of their classmates during the year. Vary the procedure used to assign places from drawing names out of a hat to various sociometric procedures to teacher assignment procedures. But do give special attention to seating children with poor eyesight and hearing, and to children with poor study habits. Make sure these pupils are not improperly placed in any assignment procedure you follow.

DIRECT ROOM TRAFFIC INTELLIGENTLY

When pupils aren't seated, they're usually standing, and when they're standing, they're usually moving. It's rather foolish to plan seating arrangements without carefully considering room traffic patterns.

Plan room traffic by thinking in terms of through streets and side streets. Arrange room furniture so that pupils can easily get to and walk along the through streets (or wide aisles). This will discourage traffic in narrow areas between desks. The through room traffic arterials should take pupils to the outside doors, to the drinking fountain, the teacher's desk, to the room's reference books, and to any other areas used frequently.

In the room arrangement suggested above, each pair of tables adjoins a wide aisle that takes pupils directly to the front or back of the room. But the staggered desk arrangement makes it more difficult to move to the sides of the room. Side movement in a classroom is more noticeable to pupils facing forward, and therefore, it is more distracting. Forward or backward movement is in the line of sight of most pupils and so is not as noticeable and distracting.

It's better to divide the aisle area available into a few wide aisles than into many narrow ones. Narrow aisles lead to horseplay between pupils walking and pupils sitting, and to books and papers inadvertently brushed to the floor.

If possible, arrange furniture and storage areas so that the pupils' traffic moves toward the back of the room initially rather than toward the front. For example, if a pupil needs to look up something in a reference work, it would be better to have him go to the back of the room and look it up. While he is walking to the back of the room he will have his mission on his mind, and so he will be less inclined toward horseplay. While he is returning to his desk, he will see only the backs of his classmates' heads and not their faces, and this also should cut down on the mischief.

Only one person at a time should be allowed to go to an area or device that can be used by only one person, such as the drinking fountain, the pencil sharpener, or the sink. Reduce the number of such trips pupils take. Discourage constant pencil sharpening trips by asking pupils to sharpen dull pencils before school begins. Place a reminder sign near the door before school begins. Ask pupils to keep waste paper until they go out for recess. Place the wastepaper basket near the door. Use room monitors to hand out books and collect written assignments.

This doesn't mean that pupils shouldn't move around at all. It's far better to have them move about occasionally than to have them sit and squirm in their seats. Teachers rarely sit still for an hour, and so they often don't realize that their pupils have been sitting reasonably still for quite a length of time. But arrange activities so that room movement is somewhat controlled and you won't have to contend with a lot of random and unnecessary movement.

Restroom traffic poses special problems. Since some pupils are embarrassed by any elaborate permission requirements, limit or eliminate these, and make the exit as unnoticed as possible. Because it's not generally wise to have more than one boy and one girl out at a time, you might construct a little in-out sign for boys and girls near the door so that others can see whether it's all right to leave the room. At the beginning of the year agree on a time limit for pupils to be out of the room. If some pupils misuse these agreements, deal with them privately.

The mass movement of an entire class also causes special problems. Groups should always walk on the right side of the corridor. They should never walk in a formation that is too wide to pass through a door. Usually, two abreast works well. You might consider walking at the front of the line while going and at the back of the line while returning. Most pupils are eager to go somewhere and will stay together while they are going there. Also, you should be present at the front to lead them through the correct doors, get permissions, and ask information when necessary. Since returning pupils are more apt to straggle your presence at the end of the line should keep the line moving together.

SCHEDULE ACTIVITIES CAREFULLY

Beginning teachers worry about how they're going to keep a room full of pupils occupied six hours a day for 180 days. Experienced teachers know that the six hours isn't one continuous block of time, but rather several smaller segments of time they schedule sequentially. They organize these shorter segments within a framework of regularly scheduled breaks in the school day, such as recess periods, milk breaks, and lunch. In addition, they further divide these segments and vary activities within them on the basis of things they have learned about the physical and mental development of children. Through careful and imaginative handling of a routine schedule, they can make the six hours pass swiftly for themselves and their classes.

Effective and imaginative scheduling implies that the teacher thinks big and schedules small. Thinking big means that you should be able to summarize in a sentence or two what you plan to accomplish in a year in each of the time segments you establish. Suppose someone asks you what you plan to do with the ninety hours you have assigned to arithmetic. If you're a third grade teacher you might reply that your major concern is to develop in your pupils a clear understanding of the fundamental generalization that every arithmetic problem they will face in life is nothing more than a search to equalize the two sides of an equation; addition, subtraction, multiplication, and division are merely the tools we use to find what equals $4 + 3$, 15×6, or any other equation.

Scheduling small means that when you teach you break these larger generalizations into smaller more specific areas of study and assign a portion of the ninety hours to each. For example, in the illustration above you would certainly want to explore the notion of equality and inequality with your class. And you would certainly want to assign time for explorations of ways in which multiplication can be used to speed up the solution of problem situations that your pupils formerly solved with addition procedures. How much time you will spend on each of these and other aspects of a major objective is a decision you will have to make on the basis of curriculum requirements and the maturity and ability of your class.

A good schedule is not a happenstance production. It is carefully developed on the basis of a realistic appraisal of time, space, and human relationships that exist in a classroom. Below are several such factors you should consider as you develop a schedule for your classroom.

Good schedules are balanced. They organize instruction so that pupils use all their sense organs and learn through a variety of procedures. As you establish the framework for your classes, alternate activities that are normally sedentary with activities that permit movement, alternate individual study with group work, and alternate activities that normally require a lot of writing with activities that are primarily oral. Pupils should have opportunities to work alone and in groups, to listen and to talk, to manipulate objects and to see pictures. Constant study of class and curriculum should lead you to a careful selection and blending and ordering of activities that will maintain high interest.

Good schedules consider the class and the classroom. Take a long, hard look at your working conditions. Consider carefully the age level and experiential characteristics of your class, their attention span, their maturity, their abilities, and their weaknesses. Cast a critical eye on the weather, the desks, a noisy lawnmower operating outside your window on Wednesday afternoons, and the amount of noise that comes from the hall when classes move along it. And then arrange your schedule to take advantage of the good, and to minimize the damage of the bad.

Good schedules consider the teacher's strengths and weaknesses. While it's wrong to ride your hobby horses to the exclusion or real detriment of other responsibilities, it's also wrong to refuse pupils their right to see you at your best, teaching those areas you like and know and can teach best. For example, if your are interested in geology, spend time on it during the year. Your pupils will probably run across few teachers interested in this subject during their schooling. What a pity if you wouldn't make the best of your opportunity. Time and schedule suggestions in your local and state guides are usually not so inflexible that they can't be adjusted to take advantage of teachers' special interests and abilities.

Good schedules take advantage of natural breaks during the day, recesses, milk breaks, lunch hour, and the like. Think in terms of larger blocks of time that take up the time between two such natural breaks, and insert your social studies or arithmetic or language arts activities in these blocks of time. It doesn't make much difference what time of the day you teach arithmetic or spelling or any other subject, although some teachers insist there is a best time of the day for some subjects. The way the subject is taught is much more important than its position on the schedule.

Good schedules are flexible. Be willing to adjust your schedule as conditions arise. More than that, arrange conditions so that changes are desirable and necessary from time to time. It will add variety and sparkle to the day. A periodic wholesale shift of the schedule adds interest when things get too bogged down in routine. How many teachers have ever started the day off with art or music or physical education? Heresy? Hardly. Why not try it some time?

The schedule is not an end in itself. It is nothing more than a framework that saves unnecessary effort and decision on the part of the teacher and class each day. And as such, it can be arranged in an almost infinite variety of ways. Don't let it rule you and your class. Rather, arrange it so that it serves you.

COOPERATE IN HOUSEKEEPING CHORES

Reinhold Marxhausen, the artist, once told of an experience he had at college. He lived several blocks from school but walked the distance daily. From almost the first day he couldn't help but notice that one block of the much-used stretch of street was much cleaner than the others. By chance he made his trip a little earlier one morning. He saw a well dressed older lady out policing up that particular block. She had a broom and a rake and a basket, and she picked up all the cigarette butts, the ice cream sticks, the gum wrappers, and the other trappings of our advanced civilization that she found littering the area. She was responsible for none of this rubbish. But she picked it up. She cleaned her block with no thought of reward or recognition, but only from a strong desire to help keep her small part of a large metropolitan area uncluttered. Mr. Marxhausen found himself emulating her as he continued his daily trips. He often arrived at school with a sack full of litter. She had won a convert.

When a person buys a package of gum or a pack of cigarettes or a candy bar or a popsicle, he buys the entire package—what he wants and also the wrapping. So often people take the part they want and enjoy, and then discard the rest on the street or floor. Is that fair? Is it fair for a person to enjoy his candy bar or cigarette and then let the rest of society live with the accumulated, unsightly refuse of self-centered persons like himself? I should hope not!

Teachers have a special challenging responsibility to develop in their pupils a sense of what that woman was fighting for, an unlittered and relatively neat patch of earth on which to live. Coaches sense the importance of neatness when they require their teams to travel to games dressed in shirts and ties. They realize that the person who has a little pride in his appearance is a little better for it. It's a plus factor in living that doesn't require much work and effort really, but that returns big dividends in the development of responsible citizens, citizens who have a little pride in themselves and in their communities.

Don't let the fact that your school has a custodian keep you from involving your class in custodian chores. Your pupils have a responsibility to help clean up whatever mess they caused. They shouldn't continue through life secure in the knowledge that someone will always clean up after them.

Enlist the entire class in housekeeping chores. Determine with your class those activities that everyone can do every day and those that should be delegated to individuals. Then work out some type of orderly procedure for delegating the second type so that everyone participates equally during the year.

Each pupil should be responsible for his desk and the area immediately adjacent. These areas ought to be clean at recess breaks, at noon, and before the pupils are dismissed at the end of the day. Each pupil should be responsible for the proper storage of his coat, his hat, and his overshoes. Pupils who bring their lunches should not be allowed to litter the school with remains.

Construct a chart with all names listed alphabetically. Cut in slots before each name so that assignment cards can be placed in these slots. It's a good idea to make assignments for a week at a time. Print the assignments on little cards and move the cards down the list, one name each week. Consider skipping a name between cards so that a person is on one week and off the next. When a card gets to the bottom of the list, start it over again at the top.

The list of housekeeping chores will vary from room to room, but it will probably include some of the following:

Dust the window sills	Water the flowers
Dust the piano	Feed any animals in the room
Clean the chalk troughs	Arrange the reference books properly
Empty the pencil sharpener	Tidy up storage areas
Clean off the sink	Erase the chalkboards

What goes for pupils also goes for teachers. Notice, nothing was said about the teacher's desk. That's your responsibility. And unless you can keep your desk reasonably clean, you won't be able to implement any pupil-operated housekeeping program successfully.

KEEP YOUR RECORDS STRAIGHT AND UP-TO-DATE

Teachers are tired at the end of the school day. By the time they have had a fast cup of coffee in the faculty lounge, plunged into the remains of one day and the preparations for the next, and filled a briefcase with papers to correct at home, they are happy to leave. And when they leave their classroom, they leave that day behind them forever.

The chances are, though, that something worth remembering and recording happened that day. And the chances are good that it will be forgotten in a few days as new events and problems vie for their attention. When teachers sign a contract to teach, they also agree to evaluate and summarize and record any data about their pupils that might prove valuable in later conferences with parents, principals, and psychologists; that may help succeeding teachers in their work with these pupils; and that may help a principal write a letter of transfer or recommendation years later. Record keeping is a task many teachers think they can get to next week or next month, but it can't be done properly that way.

Record keeping is an everyday task because events worth recording occur every day. If ever a day would come when nothing worth recording occurred, that fact would be worth recording.

It's really not difficult and time consuming to keep a daily record of raw information that can later be summarized and incorporated into cumulative files. It takes a few minutes at most. Most teachers who dread bringing files up-to-date at the end of the year dread it because they have forgotten more about the year than they remember. But perhaps the best reason for continuous record-keeping is the use a teacher can make of his data *during* the year. Periodic study of this information will suggest any changes in procedure with individual pupils and with the entire class that appear to be necessary. Develop a simple system for gathering and recording information about your class, and then use it.

One form that is relatively simple to keep is described in Figure 5. Duplicate enough copies so you'll have one for each day of the school year (or half the year if your school transfers many pupils during the year). Include pupils' names on the duplicated form to save that daily

Column 1: T – Tardy, A – Absent, A.M. P.M.

Column 2: Check if assignments due today were uncompleted at end of day.

Column 3: Any unusually strong emotional state: H – Happy, D – Depressed, A – Argumentative, C – Cooperative, U – Uncooperative

DATE	NAME	1	2	3	HEALTH	ADDITIONAL INFORMATION
10-6	FRANK BAKER	T am	—	D	SORE THROAT	
10-6	BETTY CARLSON		✓	A		HAD AN ARGUMENT WITH SUSAN AND LYNN
10-6	JIM FRANKS		—	CH		FATHER RETURNING FROM EXTENDED TRIP
10-6	MARY GREEN	A	—	—	MEASLES	
10-6	LINDA MANN		—	—		GAVE GOOD REPORT

Figure 5.

73

effort. Leave space for pupils who enter later in the year. Develop your own set of categories and system of coding to meet your particular teaching situation. At the end of each day fill in pertinent information behind the appropriate names.

Re-examine these at the end of each week and month to discover trends and patterns. Then, at the end of the month cut them into strips and staple or paste each pupil's strips in sequence on a sheet of paper. This will give you a quick view of each pupil's records for the month. Insert these pasted sheets in the pupil's file for later examination at grading times and at other times when information on the pupil is sought.

You can get a more subjective and general picture of the year by keeping a diary of the school year. At the end of each day record your observations of the day in narrative form. Write of incidents and impressions as you see them in your mind after the last good-bye has been said each day.

Keep a room diary. Assign a different pupil each day to make the entry. He should report events as he saw them during that day. He should also include any decisions and appointments and accomplishments made during the day. These entries make interesting reading, especially towards the end of the year. Pupils will refer to the diary often to settle disputes over things that happened earlier in the year, to recall how something was decided, and just to muse over events long past.

Consider also intensive observation of individual children. Select a pupil each day and pay particular attention to his activities that day. Note typical and atypical behavior. At the end of the day record your observations and include the paper in his file. During the school year you should have about six such observations on each pupil. These are particularly useful during parent-teacher conferences.

On the last day of each month ask pupils to write a brief paper on the month just ended. Ask them to record their impressions of high and low points, of problems and solutions. Collect these and file them in pupils' folders after you've read them. These observations often provide guidance towards improvements in classroom inter-relationships. Refer to these papers again at the end of the year when you summarize the year in the cumulative records.

Record-keeping devices such as these take up relatively little time if you arrange things so that the work is included in your normal working schedule. Constant observation and recording will sharpen your ability to see and evaluate pupil behavior that accurately anticipates and describes positive and negative aspects of pupils' personalities. You will be a better teacher for it.

4

TEACH FOR
REAL LEARNING

TEACH IMAGINATIVELY
AND INTERESTINGLY

A teacher may be a pleasant person to know, but he isn't much of a teacher unless he can capture and hold the attention of pupils when he teaches. This doesn't mean he must be a clown and tell jokes and do tricks to keep things lively. Actually, his best attention getting and holding device is sound and imaginative teaching of an interesting subject—and almost any subject can be made interesting.

A teacher should approach the pupil and the subject he is teaching from several angles. First, he should consider the imagination, the intellect, and the conduct of the pupil. Second, matching these aspects, he should bear in mind that the subject he teaches has (1) a bit of romance about it, (2) an intellectually conceived order or arrangement of sorts, and (3) it involves generalizations that have wide application to life. Good classroom relations result from imaginative teaching that is a subtle blend of these two parallel sets of three factors, now emphasizing one, now another, now combining both. Let's briefly examine the two sets to discover how they can be used to improve instruction.

Imagination and romance: What is the essence of the subject that struck the imagination of researchers, scholars, and explorers who spent their lives studying the subject? Have you ever wondered, during

77

a Business-Education Day tour, how people can devote their lives to the development and marketing of such things as irrigation pipes or candy bars or cross pieces for telephone poles? These people speak earnestly of their product. They are convinced it is the best on the market, and that the world is a better place because of it. Somehow, they have discovered romance in cross pieces for telephone poles. It has engaged their imagination just as surely as outer space has engaged the imagination of space scientists.

Storytelling is the teacher's best avenue to the pupils' imagination. Pupils are more apt to identify themselves with a subject and discover romance in it if they can do it through the life of someone who got excited about it and followed his dream. The study of rockets becomes much more exciting if it is studied through the successes and failures of Robert Goddard. The sixth grade study of Greek and Roman history in Social Studies can become very dull if the teacher doesn't bring the heroes and poets and statesmen into the classroom. Mozart's music takes on added beauty if you know the story of his life.

Read heavily in biography and autobiography as you prepare to teach new units through the year. Encyclopedias are a quick and excellent source of leads on promising stories. Develop outlines of the stories you tell so you won't forget them the next time you teach the unit.

As you gather and organize material for teaching, keep the following questions in mind. They will help you determine where the subject itself touches the imagination of people. Then introduce the romantic aspects of the subject into your teaching at these points. You will find yourself caught up in the excitement, and you will pass it on to your class.

1. What facet of human life does this subject appeal to primarily?
2. What types of people devoted their lives to it?
3. How did they become interested in it and what held their interest?
4. What major contributions has this field made toward improving life?
5. What doors to the imagination does it open?

Intellect and order: What are the elements of the subject you are teaching, the major principles and the bits and snatches of information that constitute the body of a field of study? In what sequential or graphic order do they arrange themselves? Are all facts you teach equally important? How do the principles relate themselves to the facts?

Pupils become frustrated unless teachers indicate where each new piece of information presented fits into the scheme of things. They will find it much easier to understand and remember the operation of a squirt gun, an automobile carburetor, an atomizer, an airplane wing, and a spray gun if they are taught that all these are technical refinements of Bernoulli's principle that rapidly moving air lowers the air pressure and thereby lifts the water, gas, perfume, airplane, and paint. Multiplication tables, often presented as just a collection of facts to memorize, take on new meaning and importance when they are identified as a faster way of counting, or as an express train that stops only at regularly spaced stations (as opposed to counting by ones—a local train that stops at every station).

Below are several ways a teacher can introduce single elements of a subject into his teaching and yet show the relationship of each element to the total subject. Concern for this will help pupils gain an intellectual grasp of the system and order of every field they study.

Write the major facts or elements you plan to introduce on pieces of paper. Arrange these face down on the bulletin board in terms of the relationships (among the elements) you wish to show. You might place them in sequence, in a circular form, expanding out from a center, in rows or columns, or in some other diagrammatic form suggested by the elements. As you introduce each fact or element in your presentation, turn that sheet of paper around. When all have been thus introduced, discuss the entire set of facts in the context of the relationships you visualized with your display.

Develop a diagram that shows a relationship you want to teach. Place the skeleton of the diagram on the chalkboard before the class period begins. Fill it in during your presentation.

Seek analogies that illustrate relationships among various elements of a subject. For example, compare the functions of the various elements you are presenting to the functions of various parts of a building: The foundation, various wiring and plumbing conduits going to every part of the building, the lobby, the windows, the brick façade, the furnishings, the elevators, the people who work in the building, the visitors, and the name of the building.

Toward the end of a unit, write fifteen or so facts or elements on the board. Ask pupils to classify these in three lists: Most Important, Important, and Useful only as Background Information. Pupils' lists will vary. Use them as a springboard for a discussion on the relative importance of various elements introduced into the study.

List five or six statements, facts, or terms. Ask pupils to use them all in the construction of a paragraph that shows the relationship existing among them. For example:

> Sir Isaac Newton (1642–1727)
> "For every action there is an equal and opposite reaction."
> Robert Goddard (1882–1945)
> Jets and rockets are similar and different.
> There is no atmosphere in space.

Conduct and application: Finally, what is the significance of the subject in the lives of the pupils? How should their conduct be governed by what they have learned? Some teachers spend so much time presenting mountains of material that little or no time is left to relate it all to the real world of people beyond the most obvious and superficial use of the material. It seems such a waste to short-change the thing you've been working for all along.

Application of content to life is easiest when principles are stressed in teaching. Below are several activities that teachers can use to show pupils how to move from principles to application to their lives.

On the chalkboard write basic principles governing the subject you are teaching. Let's use Bernoulli's Principle, discussed above, as an example. Pass out pieces of paper with isolated facts and elements covered in the study, such as: The fluid in an atomizer bottle is sprayed out when the rubber bulb is squeezed. Ask pupils to read the statement they get and then relate it to the principles listed on the board.

Set up simple case studies that can be solved by the application of a principle. For example, a mechanic on a space ship must go out to repair the fuselage of his ship. As he closes the door, he discovers to his horror that he is not attached to the ship by rope. The action of closing the door causes a reaction which sends him away from his ship, slowly but surely. How can he get back to his space ship?

Arrange news stories and pictures on the bulletin board. Ask pupils to indicate principles that were employed or ignored in the activity leading to the event depicted. A rash of special sales promotions could illustrate several principles of competitive business, such as those dealing with oversupply or approaching inventory time. Scenes of traffic accidents could illustrate principles relating to speed, braking powers of cars, vision, and reflex action.

Require that class discussions and resulting decisions relate to clearly enunciated principles. Spending for a party cannot exceed income. Every member of the group has a right to be heard.

So how does this concern for imagination, intellect, and conduct in a pupil, and with romance, order, and application in a subject make a person a better teacher? It develops a closer kinship between the teacher and the pupil and the subject. It places principles and relationships in the forefront of the teacher's mind where they belong. A teacher who is caught up in the romance of a subject, who sees the system and order of the subject, and who seeks to inject these into the imagination, intellect, and lives of pupils can't help but be a better teacher for it, as well as a first class adult, one who can handle his human relations responsibilities more than adequately.

DON'T SLIGHT COMMUNICATION SKILLS

We communicate to others through various combinations of twenty-six letters and ten digits. Because of this, the language arts and arithmetic have always held a pre-eminent position in the elementary school curriculum. Almost everything else is built upon the foundation of the 3 R's.

Parents are understandably concerned about their children's success in the development of these skills. The vast amount of research carried out in these fields attests to a parallel concern of educators that pupils learn to use their language well. Indeed, your success as a teacher may rest, to a large extent, on your ability to communicate communication skills to your pupils.

One factor that hinders effective teaching and understanding of communication skills is that many teachers break them up into as many as seven discrete topics. They teach reading, writing, spelling, grammar, speaking, listening, and arithmetic as separate subjects during separate periods, and they make relatively little effort to develop in their pupils an awareness of the interrelationships that exist among the various facets of communication.

Ask yourself this question: Have you ever taught during a spelling lesson the order of letters in a four letter word, and a short time later during arithmetic the order of digits in a four place number, and indicated to your class that the communication problem inherent in the two actions was similar, that there is as big a communications difference between *hear* and *hare* as there is between *1234* and *4321?* On the other hand, have you ever expressed displeasure with your pupils for misspelling words in written work that they spelled correctly in a recent spelling test? If we don't see and teach relationships between various segments of the curriculum should we be surprised when our pupils don't either?

The size and complexity of the task we undertake when we teach pupils to communicate with each other has led to some curricular fragmentation, separate materials, and even separate teaching methods for the seven areas listed above. This places a great burden on you as a teacher to pull these separate topics together whenever possible so that your pupils can see the relationships that exist among them. The pupil who grasps the somewhat obvious relationship between careful speech and careful writing is in a position to move towards more subtle relationships such as that existing between partial products in a multiplication problem and successive drafts of a carefully written theme.

The activities suggested below should assist you in pointing out and accenting relationships that exist among the various activities you carry out as you develop communication skills in your pupils.

Many classrooms have an alphabet and number chart above the front chalkboard. Periodic reference to these thirty-six symbols as the major source of everything communicated in our society will develop in pupils an appreciation for the necessity to order and structure these symbols properly so that they communicate what we want them to communicate. It is indeed remarkable that so much can be communicated with such a small collection of items. Develop in your pupils a great respect for the versatility of our language.

Show-and-Tell Time gives primary grade teachers an excellent opportunity to develop various communications skills. Encourage pupils to tell their stories using different communications media: speaking, experience charts, chalkboard diagrams, puppetry, tape recording, riddles, overhead transparencies. Discuss with them how each of these media seeks to communicate, though through different means.

Ask pupils to work several arithmetic problems using written words instead of numbers. Discuss how much more efficient numbers are than words. Since speed in computation is desirable a separate set of symbols instead of words is used when we work with quantities. Words can be used to solve number problems but numbers cannot be used to communicate non-quantity ideas.

Ask pupils to keep an error booklet. As you call attention to the reading, writing, spelling, speaking, and grammatical errors that pupils make, they should note them in their booklets. Ask them to review their errors periodically to see if they tend to make the same errors regardless of the communication medium they use. They will discover they often do.

An interesting variation to written themes is taped themes. Ask pupils to read their themes into a tape recorder instead of turning them in in written form. Pupils should leave about a minute of tape empty between themes so that you can respond to each theme immediately after hearing it. Replay the themes and your comments to the class the next day. Discuss the difference between turning in a written theme and a spoken theme. For example, in a spoken theme punctuation is expressed through voice inflections. Written themes must express emotions through careful description while many emotions can be communicated through the voice in spoken themes. Spelling accuracy is not a factor in spoken communication but clear enunciation is.

A class newspaper can be used to draw together many communications skills. Reporters must listen to the people they interview and translate the discussion into accurate written notes which are expanded into news and feature stories. Editing requires careful attention to grammatical and spelling rules. Production requires handwriting and printing on the ditto master that will reproduce clearly and legibly. It also requires an accurate count of copies to be made. The reader must know how to attach meaning to the abstract symbols on the printed page. The experience of putting out thirty-six such issues during the year should do much to unify your teaching of communications skills, especially if you schedule a short discussion and evaluation period after each issue has come out, and if you involve all pupils in each of the several editorial and production tasks during the year. The paper will also serve as an excellent public relations medium between you and your pupils' parents. Parents will keep informed on school activities and coming events. The paper needn't be extensive. A one page dittoed weekly should be sufficient for most classes most weeks. Include drawings whenever possible.

TEACH PUPILS TO THINK VISUALLY

We are living in a world where we experience things before we read about them. When we were children we read about foreign lands and scientific wonders before we saw them. Today our children often see things on television long before they are able to read about them. When we were children we turned on the light to read. Today our children turn down the light to watch television. Our children are growing up in a world where a poor reader can be a well-informed person.

Several hundred years ago the invention of the printing press signaled the beginnings of a strong effort to achieve universal literacy. Recent advances in motion pictures and television signal an additional concern for educators, that of dealing with instant information in non-verbal terms.

The written word remains available after it is read. If something is not fully understood, it can easily be re-read and even examined in slow motion, word by word. The visual shadows of motion pictures and television disappear with the speed of light. They can be replayed and they often are, but generally not at the option of the individual viewer. This indicates that pupils must be taught to observe carefully and accurately. The parlor game of yesteryear in which a number of objects were placed on a table briefly to see how many players could recall the objects after they were removed takes on new significance in today's school.

Political campaigns and advertising have been transformed by the newer communications media. Proper lighting and correct camera angles can transform an average product or person to something outstanding in the mind of the non-discriminating viewer. Today's teachers must teach their pupils to read pictures as critically as they read words. If pupils understand such things as design, color, and balance as they relate to various art forms, they will be in a better position to judge how these are used to convey information and elicit emotional response.

Since people rarely see filmed or televised sequences more than once, it is important that they learn to view critically what they see when they see it. You can help develop such skills when you show educational films to your class. For example, films developed by private industries for classroom showing will often include subtle favorable references to the producing company and its set of values. If the film is produced by an oil company and there is a service station in the film, it will usually be an outlet of the company producing the film. The station will be clean and the service efficient. There is nothing inherently wrong with this, but pupils should be taught to notice such things.

Textbooks published today are illustrated much more profusely than they were formerly. Spend class time studying the illustrations. Help pupils learn to read them in terms of the information and emotional impact they communicate. Occasionally ask them to write out a statement that would adequately describe what is expressed in an illustration. The truth of the old adage, a picture is worth 1,000 words, will become more evident to them.

Present day teachers must think visually as they prepare their teaching presentations. You must communicate visually as well as verbally if you want to develop in your pupils the ability to read critically the vast amount of visual information that is fed to their eyes every day. For many years it has been said that teachers talk too much. Perhaps in this age that criticism takes on new meaning.

INVOLVE PUPILS IN THE LEARNING PROCESS

Two kinds of ignorance exist. The one includes those things that nobody living knows, such as the exact age of the earth, what thoughts a fish might have, and what it feels like to die. The other kind of ignorance includes those things that some people don't know, but others do, such as the Greek language, the multiplication tables, and the correct procedures for removing tonsils. The first kind of ignorance is the realm of the researcher. He ferrets out solutions to unsolved problems. When he has found a solution, he tells teachers and others about it. The teachers make it their responsibility to pass the word down the line.

This order, from researcher to teacher to pupil, places the teacher in the position of usually knowing more than the pupil. This assumed acceptance of superior knowledge can easily tempt the teacher to talk too much, to spend too much of his school time telling his pupils what he knows and they don't. Telling often seems to be the most efficient way to get the information passed down the line. We all apologize for talking too much in class, but we can all rationalize our need to do it.

Pupil involvement in many classrooms, therefore, consists primarily of pupils listening to the teacher making a presentation, reading assigned material aloud or silently, answering questions asked by the teacher, occasionally asking the teacher a question for clarification, and writing in response to the teacher's assignments. There is nothing really wrong with any of these. They are all worthy activities with a long tradition behind them. But there are also other learning activities that should be going on in the classroom.

Pupils should have opportunities to carry on discussions among themselves with the teacher serving as moderator and catalyst rather than initiator and major contributor of ideas. Pupils should have opportunities to:

1. Raise significant questions on the basis of their individual study and reading
2. Work together in small groups
3. Work individually on projects they initiate
4. Make use of all their senses in learning
5. Opportunities to think and reflect—periods of quiet during the day.

How do you stack up? It's hard to tell. It's difficult for a teacher to know how much of his teaching is a solo performance and how much is really class participation. We can't easily see ourselves and our teaching objectively.

One good way to assess your teaching is to keep a log of your

teaching from time to time. If you have access to a tape recorder, tape your teaching and make the analysis later. Otherwise, it's relatively easy to train one of your more intelligent pupils to keep a log for you. Don't try to hide such self-study from your class. Pupils react positively to teachers who constantly evaluate their teaching, and who sincerely work to improve their effectiveness.

The purpose of this log is to determine the amount of general participation in the lesson and the patterns of involvement. Did you do most of the talking? Did only a few pupils participate? What kinds of contributions did they make? Did they only answer questions? How often did you have to call on pupils to improve their behavior? Were there any sequences in which several pupils spoke in a row without you speaking?

Make three columns on sheets of ruled paper. Title them: Time—Person—Type of Statement or Activity. Use a watch with a second hand. In the first column note the (approximate) time of any change in speakers or activity. In the second column write the initials of the person who is talking. Describe the type of statement or activity in the third column using the following number code. In case the person talking makes several types of statements before another person speaks, indicate these in sequence on the same line as shown in Figure 6. Figure 6 illustrates a section of a log such as described above.

1. Explains something or lectures
2. Asks a question
3. Answers a question
4. Agrees with the previous speaker
5. Disagrees with the previous speaker
6. Gives directions
7. Asks others to behave
8. Says something that draws laughter
9. A period of relative quiet during which no one addresses the class.

Every five minutes note the general class atmosphere, whether: (A) excited and eager about the lesson, (B) attentive, (C) apathetic, (D) belligerent. Use the letters.

Study these logs carefully. Note patterns of participation. Compute the number of times and the amount of time you talked. Do the same

TIME	PERSON	TYPE OF STATEMENT OR ACTIVITY
1:00	TEACHER	7,6
1:02	BL	2
1:02:30	TEACH.	3,1,2
1:05	CLASS	B
1:09	GM	3
1:09:15	TEACH,	5,2
1:09:30	GMC	3,8
1:09:50	TEACH	4,7,1
1:10	CLASS	C

Figure 6.

for class members. Note any discussions carried on among class members without your participation. What triggered these exchanges? Where could you have involved pupils more than you did? If you were to teach the period over again, what changes would you make? Discuss your tabulations and assessments with your class. Get their reactions.

A class period is not more valuable just because many pupils participated. Many Arizona pupils could participate in a discussion on life in a tropical rain forest, but their participation would probably not be nearly as valuable as an extended statement by a person who had actually lived in one. Class participation is valuable when the discussion is so structured that pupils' knowledge and experience can be used to gain an understanding of things they don't know. Don't apologize for sharing your greater knowledge and experience with your class. But don't bungle opportunities to show them how they can use their more limited knowledge and experience to gain more knowledge. Use your experiences when you must. Use theirs whenever you can.

LEAD EFFECTIVE CLASS DISCUSSIONS

As indicated above, well-executed class discussions are rare commodities, from kindergarten through college. Yet, democracy depends partly for its survival upon the individual's ability to participate effectively in group decision and action. Teachers at all levels should consider the development of discussion skills a major responsibility.

An effective discussion is composed of several elements. There is an implied belief that the knowledge sought resides within the pooled knowledge and experience of the group. Participants follow certain procedures designed to bring out the best contributions of each in an orderly manner. They also play a number of roles as the discussion weaves its way to solution of the problem. Established procedures are employed at the point of formal or informal decision. In developing discussion skills, teachers typically concentrate on the procedure and decision functions of group action and say little of the role-playing functions and the significance of this interplay in good group relations.

Pupils are somewhat surprised to discover that participants in a discussion play a large number of roles besides those of chairman and secretary. They have witnessed the enactment of these various roles many times, and have possibly played most of them themselves, but they have not thought of these as roles that are enacted with surprising regularity in all sorts of discussions. Effective participation arises from an understanding of the interplay of various discussion roles. These have been identified in sophisticated terms by writers in group dynamics. The listing below has been developed for unsophisticated younger people who also need to know about these roles. Use this list as you develop discussion skills with your class. Tape class discussions and replay them in order to analyze with your class various roles played. Use the form described earlier and the categories listed below to keep a log of class discussion. Teach your pupils to play positive roles in class discussions, and to identify and resist manipulation from persons playing negative roles.

DISCUSSION ROLES FROM A TO Z:

- People who help move the discussion forward to a positive solution:
    - A. Seek facts that would answer a question or problem raised.
    - B. Supply the facts sought.
    - C. Show how these facts relate to the purpose of the discussion.
    - D. Show how these facts relate to points previously mentioned.
    - E. Suggest new approaches or new ways of looking at things when the discussion gets bogged down.
    - F. Try to combine several suggestions into something all can agree to.
    - G. Encourage the group to come to a decision.

- People who don't move the discussion forward, but rather help hold it at an even keel while participants work their way through a temporary deadlock:
    - H. Seek opinions of others instead of facts.
    - I. Give their opinion in response to request.
    - J. Question whether a suggestion will work as claimed.
    - K. Clear the air briefly with a joke when strong disagreements develop.
    - L. Suggest the group re-study its goal or purpose.
    - M. Suggest that some who haven't said anything express their views.
    - N. Indicate that they will go along with whatever the rest decide.

- People who perform certain jobs for the group:
    - O. Serve as group leader or chairman.
    - P. Serve as group secretary or recorder.
    - Q. Perform odd jobs such as opening windows or turning on the lights.

- People who slow down or actually destroy the discussion:
    - R. Make speeches instead of briefly expressing their views.
    - S. Seem to be against everything suggested, though they offer nothing themselves.
    - T. Try to dominate the whole discussion by claiming they alone have the background and information to make the proper decision.
    - U. Brag about themselves and what they have done.
    - V. Interrupt others who are speaking.
    - W. Try to get their way by telling of the hardships that will

come to them if the group decides against their position.
X. Play around and poke fun during the discussion.
Y. Talk about things that have nothing to do with the discussion topic.
Z. Use their position as boss, supervisor, or teacher to get the group to see things their way in situations where the group should decide freely.

DEVELOP RESPONSIBILITY THROUGH COMMITTEE WORK

Much inept committee performance in school can be traced to poor human relations resulting from a lack of clearly defined procedures. Often, one committee member or a small clique attempts to dominate discussions with pet ideas and preconceived solutions. Antagonism almost always develops. Flunky work is often assigned to quiet and retiring members while the dramatic work and plaudits are taken by the more outgoing. Smouldering resentment results. Petty arguments consume more and more time. Absenteeism and apathy appear. Goals are not reached because they weren't clearly defined or else have been long forgotten. The final report to the class or club is poorly prepared and presented. What should have been a positive contribution is a disappointment. It shouldn't happen that way, and it doesn't have to.

Effective and satisfying committee action is certainly much more complex than following a few procedures, but problems such as those indicated above often develop when procedures are not clearly defined and followed, Therefore, teachers who are unsuccessful in working with class committees might well be advised to begin by establishing a framework of procedures that encourage success. Effective procedures are common sense procedures that equalize committee contributions and commendations while keeping the objective clearly in mind. Pupils who learn during their school years that common sense procedures yield maximum results with a minimum of wasted effort and ragged nerves will want to follow these procedures in adult life.

The best time to develop skills needed in committee activity is during class unit work such as that carried on in science and social studies classes. The teacher controls committee assignments and the focus of activity. Time allotments are somewhat flexible. All pupils in the class are involved. All are working on similar problems at about the same time.

Let's assume it is toward the beginning of the year, and your class is starting a unit on electricity. You have decided to carry out certain presentations yourself, but you would like pupils to prepare and present others. One group will study and report on the nature of electricity. Other groups will study and report on ways of generating electricity, turning electricity into light and heat, electric motors, famous scientists who worked with electricity, and future uses of electricity. Each group will meet together an hour a day for five or six days to prepare its report.

Given the opportunity, school groups will often fritter away too much time and energy getting organized, electing a whole host of non-essential officers, and selecting a name for their committee. In addition, they will ask permission to meet in the cloakroom, library, cafeteria, restroom, or any other place sufficiently removed from your vision and hearing. They will begin their deliberations with a long and often disorderly discussion of the format and mechanics of their final report with relatively little thought of its content. And the interpersonal problems indicated earlier often follow shortly.

Instead, teach them how to proceed systematically, to get maximum returns for each minute spent. Begin with the first meeting after the groups have been formed by choice or chance. Spend the first ten minutes or so helping the groups plan an agenda for their first meeting. Write the agenda on the board. First order of business should be the selection of a chairman and secretary. Indicate several procedures they might follow if necessary. Second order of business should be an exploratory discussion of the subject to be studied. This should result in a consensus of the scope of the study and identification of areas to be investigated first. Third order of business should be the specific assignment of duties to each member of the committee to be carried out prior to the next meeting. Such things as availablity of sources, answers to questions raised, definitions, and additional background material should be investigated.

Committees should meet in different sections of the classroom the first day. Allow but thirty minutes for the meeting so the groups will get right to work. Move about constantly to make sure each group is proceeding through the agenda. Some suggestions can be given to groups that bog down on this or that point, but it's better to help them seek their own solutions. Note potential interpersonal problems in groups. Quite often these can be handled quietly with a few words to the individuals involved later on in the day.

At the conclusion of the period, pupils should return to their desks. Secretaries should report briefly to the class on their committees' deliberations and decisions. Groups are more apt to concentrate on their assignments if they know they have to report on their progress at the end of each work period. In addition, these daily progress reports take some of the pressure off the final report which is rarely as effective a report as teachers would like it to be.

Help the groups set up an agenda the second day also. Reports from each committee member should be the first order of business. Each member must carry out his assigned responsibility if the group is to function properly. Second order of business should be the utilization of this information in the development of the framework within which the succeeding work will be done and around which the final report will be written. Normally, this framework can be determined by school groups in two meetings, but some groups may need additional meetings. Final order of business should be the assignment of an area of responsibility to each member.

Again, the last part of the period should be used to hear reports from each committee. An important part of each committee report should be a clear statement of the scope of the investigation. Encourage class discussion of problems faced by the various groups. Seek solutions to common problems. Spend some time discussing individual and group responsibilities in the days ahead. Try to instill a desire to present an excellent report based on an excellent piece of research. In order to get this across, you will have to make sure that your own contributions and class presentations are also first rate.

Succeeding periods will be spent in a variety of individual and group activities as committees carry out their investigations. A few minutes should be spent at the beginning of each period, however, to allow each chairman to indicate what his group will do that day. Brief reports should also be given at the end of each period indicating what was actually accomplished. Meet with each group periodically to give guidance and to help evaluate progress. Schedule meetings with the chairmen to discuss problems and help them develop agendas and time schedules. Individual meetings with the chairmen should result in more equalized work loads for members of the committees and suggestions for solving interpersonal problems that develop. Don't be afraid to require responsible behavior from those who have been assigned responsibility. This is as much a function of your position as teacher as it is a function of each committee secretary to keep accurate minutes.

As groups complete their investigations, they should report to the class. The reports should be complete, concise, informative, and interesting. A complete written report should be given to you the day before the presentation. The report should be read and signed by each member of the group, to insure that the written report actually reflects the consensus of the committee members. It should include the following information:

1. A brief summary of the work of the committee. This should be written by the secretary and based on her minutes.
2. A statement listing specific assignments and contributions of each member of the committee. This should be written by the chairman.
3. A bibliography listing materials actually used in the study.
4. A complete description of the report to be given in class.

The day after the report is given, each member should submit a written evaluation of what he personally believed to be the strengths and weaknesses of his committee's work and report.

As indicated earlier, this will not solve all problems associated with class committee work and guarantee success, but it will go a long way toward improving the quality of the work done, and this in itself should resolve many of the other problems before they arise. Problems arising from petty considerations tend to disappear when the eye is kept on larger things.

MAKE STUDY PERIODS *STUDY* PERIODS

Study the fifteen digits below for fifteen seconds. Then try to write them from memory before going on to the next paragraph.

1 4 9 1 6 2 5 3 6 4 9 6 4 8 1

How did you do? Most people don't do too well. They panic at the thought of trying to do so much in so little time that they waste what little time they have. People who score well on tests such as this organize their time for maximum returns. They seek relationships among numbers instead of trying to memorize fifteen separate digits. They know they can memorize a relationship in just a few seconds and remember it, but that it would take much longer to memorize a long series of digits, and then they would soon forget it.

Is there such a relationship in the series of digits above? Yes, there is. Starting from the left (with some combining) the digits are the square of one, the square of two, the square of three . . . and so on up to the square of nine. It's easy to remember the series of fifteen digits now, isn't it?

This little test illustrates a major problem facing the teacher concerned with developing study skills in pupils. Fifteen seconds or fifteen minutes, the principles of effective study are the same. Pupils are often inclined to study material without considering its organization, major emphases, or relationships existing within the material. In addition, much of their studying is done in group situations fraught with distractions. Teachers must help pupils develop effective study habits if pupils are expected to use study periods effectively.

The first thing a teacher can do is to make the classroom conducive to study. Minimize distractions as much as possible. Don't permit pupils to wander aimlessly about the room during study periods. Keep a supply of sharpened pencils available for trading purposes in order to keep the pencil sharpener quiet. If a group must meet during the period, or if you want to talk at length with a pupil, do it in the rear of the room where it will be less distracting. Each distraction has a solution if you put your mind to it.

Most people have clocks built into their systems. Plan study periods accordingly within time limits geared to the maturity of the pupils. Pupils will be more apt to work right up to the end of a study period that was planned intelligently. As they develop study skills, they will be more able to work effectively with more flexible time limits. At the beginning of a study period, ask pupils to plan their study and indicate on a scrap of paper how long they plan to work on each item. Tell them to place their paper on their desk where you can see it as you move about the room. It will help you identify those who have difficulty establishing and holding to a schedule. In addition, it will help pupils work toward shorter goals. A thirty minute study period seems forbidding but a five minute segment doesn't. Some pupils may resist such planning at first, but they will continue the practice on their own after a while, when they discover its benefits.

When the entire class is to work on the same material during a study period, spend some time organizing the period together so that study is concentrated on the subject. Point out major issues and relationships presented in the material. On the board write several questions relating to these major issues. Ask pupils to write answers on a sheet of paper. Move about the room and quietly note the progress of the class. Help those who need help. Discuss the questions and their answers at the close of the study period.

Much study time is spent reading textbooks. Yet, many pupils read textbooks inefficiently. Perhaps the best approach to studying textbooks is the SQ3R Method. Teach it to your pupils.

SURVEY: Spend a minute or two glancing through the chapter to discover the major points that are developed. Pay special attention to the headings, illustrations, diagrams, and the like that call attention to the major ideas. Read the summary paragraph at the end of the chapter if it has one. From this you should gain a good idea of what to expect when you read the chapter.

QUESTION: Now begin to read. Turn the first section heading into a question. If it says, Boyle Discovers an Important Principle of Breathing, the obvious question is, "What principle did Boyle discover?" The question should arouse the reader's curiosity and bring to mind information already known.

READ: Read to find the answer to that question. This gives purpose to reading. Pupils often read material passively. They read the words because each word gets them a little closer to the end of the chapter. This procedure stops that and encourages more purposeful reading.

RECITE: Look away from the book after the section is completed and answer the question in your mind. Use your own words and add an example from your own experience if possible. Jot down the major point learned from the question and answer.

Repeat the question, read, and recite steps on each succeeding section.

REVIEW: When the chapter is read, read through your notes to see if you understand the major points and relationships discussed. Then glance through the chapter again. Turn each section heading into a question, and then answer it without re-reading the section.

You might think the above suggestions take too much effort. Some teachers consider study periods a good time to catch up with correcting papers, planning lessons, or even resting. It is good to remember, though, that pupils will put the same value on study periods that you do. They won't consider them important if you don't. And if you don't consider them important, your troubles have just begun.

COOPERATE WITH ALL YOUR PUPILS' TEACHERS

In our society formal education takes place in classrooms removed from the hustle and bustle of the adult workaday world. In the past society was represented by one teacher charged with instilling Western civilization into his charges.

In recent years there have been increasing pressures to bring additional teachers into your classroom. How should you react to such intrusions as: educational television, teaching machines and other forms of programmed learning, taped lessons for language labs, a greatly expanded number and variety of teaching films and filmstrips including single concept films that can take much of the drudgery out of skill teaching, teacher aids who can free you from routine tasks, special teachers for individual pupils who need help, and special teachers to help you with your entire class in areas where your teaching competence is limited?

You must begin by separating in your mind those teachers who are physically present in your room, such as a music teacher, and those who are not, such as the person who programmed the programmed textbook your pupils might use. Two different types of human relations problems are involved.

Teachers who are physically present: You have an obligation to prepare your pupils to work effectively with any other teachers who will work with them during the year. You should meet such teachers and discuss with them such matters as behavior expectations, routine procedures established for class movement and participation, and your presence or absence in the room during such periods. Then prepare your pupils for these other teachers. If the special teacher prefers to work in an atmosphere that is different from that which normally exists in your room, your pupils should be appraised of this and their cooperation enlisted. Do not say or do anything that will undercut such teachers with your pupils by implying to your pupils that something extraordinary is being asked of them. Within a few years they will work with a different teacher each hour in high school and each of these teachers may have a different set of expectations. At the same time you should serve as a buffer between your class and any unreasonable demands made by special teachers. Any such problems should be discussed away from the pupils, however.

Teachers who are not physically present: It's still somewhat early to know what effect such "mechanical" teachers as programmers and ETV studio teachers will have on classroom human relations. Feedback is important in communication, and most of these approaches have not adequately solved the problem of communication from pupil to teacher. The pupil using programmed materials makes a response and the programmer indicates (in advance) whether or not the response is correct, but this seems dissatisfying to pupils over any length of time—just as we were dissatisfied when our college themes and tests were corrected by readers and not by the professors we met in class.

Some ETV studio teachers make a real attempt to make personal visits to schools that receive their programs, and they should be commended for their efforts, but even such meetings are not always conducive to the interchange of questions pupils might have since time is usually limited and several grades meet together in an assembly room.

It would seem that the classroom teacher should step into any such mechanical instruction at the point where the pupil wants to react. In the case of programmed materials you should schedule periodic discussion periods with pupils who are using the materials. These discussions should move your pupils beyond the factual material in the program and relate it to real and specific problems they face. Unless you do this you will have no way of knowing if pupils can make the transfer from the programmed material to their own life.

ETV offers more opportunities for a closer relationship with the teacher. The studio teacher is not as anonymous as a programmer. Pupils develop a good two-dimensional image of the teacher through repeated viewings. You can pump blood into that image by encouraging pupils to write letters to the teacher, by making efforts to meet the teacher, and possibly by scheduling a field trip to the studio from which he works. Televised lessons should be properly introduced and discussed. Pupils should not consider them relatively harmless interludes in the school day. If mechanically transmitted teaching is to be of value, you will have to help make it so.

5

SEE THE INDIVIDUAL CAPACITY
OF EACH PUPIL

RECOGNIZE INDIVIDUAL DIFFERENCES

Several years ago a superior high school teacher I knew made a somewhat surprising change in teaching positions; he left a well-paying position in a wealthy suburb to accept, at less salary, a teaching position in a small lumber community. He said he felt more like a servant than a teacher in the wealthy suburb. He couldn't even afford to live there. He lived in a less exclusive neighboring community along with the tradesmen and service people who maintained the wealthy suburb. His patrons considered him a skilled technician who was adequately paid for his efforts. He felt that many of his pupils didn't really need him. Their financial future was already assured without his help. He was useful to them in that his teaching skill could help them get into the "right" college. His pupils were clean, well-behaved, friendly, and tolerant of their teachers. They knew their teachers were below their socio-economic level. He felt important to the community in the same way the garbage collector was important; the community couldn't get along without the service, but the man supplying it could be readily replaced from a long line of applicants. He was unhappy in a school system considered excellent by most teachers.

Many parents in the lumber community wanted their children to leave the community when they grew up. Few fathers wanted their

sons to follow them into the mill or woods. Lacking money to help
their children, they looked to their community's teachers as a way out
and up for their children. If only their children could get the education
they themselves missed; if only their children could get scholarships; if
only their children would develop the incentive to make something of
themselves; then these parents could realize their own unfulfilled
dreams in their children. In that community, good teachers were
accorded real respect because they came few and far between. Since
he was a good teacher, he found himself recognized and greeted on the
street and in the stores. His advice was sought and followed. He was
considered a learned and important professional person, and not just a
highly trained technician. Pupils who cut-up in other classes were
respectful in his. In several respects it was frustrating to teach in such a
school and community, but he felt it was also much more satisfying to
the soul. He was happy in a school system that had difficulty attracting
and holding teachers.

This somewhat unusual and paradoxical story illustrates many of the
differences found in school life. Compare a community that offers
teachers good wages but little feeling of worth with a community that
offers respect and prestige for excellence but little money to go with it.
There are communities that offer almost anything a teacher might
desire and there are communities that offer practically nothing a
teacher might desire. Some communities measure excellence in their
schools through the quality of instruction, but others seem to measure
excellence through athletics, bands, plays and the behavior of the
students.

Compare pupils for whom high school is merely a preparatory
period for college with those for whom it represents terminal education
and others for whom it represents frustration and failure, something to
drop out of at the first chance. College-bound pupils in the two
communities described above had their sights set on different types of
colleges; and they had different reasons for wanting to go to college.
They also had different sets of anxieties. One set of pupils was
concerned about an OK from the proper admissions officer, the other
about an OK from a scholarship awards committee.

Compare a teacher who considers community prestige a rightful and
important part of his remuneration with another teacher who considers

the size of his salary the sincerest form of community respect for his ability. Compare a teacher who considers himself as much a professional person as a doctor or lawyer with another teacher who considers himself a well trained and skilled technician. Compare career teachers with teachers who teach primarily to get a second pay check into the family fortunes.

Some would suggest that the teacher described above isn't really a superior teacher because his motives are wrong. Others would argue that motives are immaterial. To gain and hold community prestige he would have to produce results, and produce he did with a glittering record of scholarship winners among his former pupils. Still others would not make scholarships the criterion of teaching excellence, even in a community where these were almost essential if a pupil wanted to go to college. Some would call him a fool for not staying in a school that had the facilities and the resources to make best use of his considerable talents, and that would pay him properly. Others would praise him for his willingness to work among those who most needed teaching excellence, but who were least able to pay for it.

These differences of opinion make for good faculty coffee room discussions, because no one is right and no one is wrong. At least, it's hard to prove it.

[We are unique. As pupils and teachers we have such a complex combination of characteristics and motives that it's better to begin our acquaintance with others as they are when we meet them, than it is to point the finger of scorn too readily] It's better to accept the teacher described above for what he is, if he would become your colleague, than it is to begin your relationship by either impugning or praising his motives. It's better to accept the community and school where you agreed to teach for what they are than it is to try to re-make them, before the first snow falls, into your image of what a community and school should be. Welcome the tremendous variability you face in every teaching situation in which you find yourself; accept variability as an elementary fact of life, and don't try to force everything you meet into a mold of your making.

Does that mean that teachers shouldn't be instruments of change? No, it doesn't. [Teachers should work for change wherever it is needed. But the teacher who recognizes individual differences makes a sincere attempt to understand the reasons for variant conditions before he suggests modifications. And he tries to effect change within the context of the uniqueness of the situation whenever possible. For example, he knows that each pupil brings a unique matrix of background and ability and interest with him to school. Since these factors bear on learning, the pupil's uniqueness will influence his learning. Similarly, future learning will increase his uniqueness. The wise teacher will seek ways of awakening each pupil to his own uniqueness and to the uniqueness of others. He will help each pupil develop skills of self-evaluation that will help him change what needs to be changed, and retain what should be retained, and to learn the difference between the two.

IDENTIFY DIFFERENCES AMONG PUPILS

Grouping pupils generally poses problems for teachers, primarily problems of human relations. For example, it's not difficult to identify fast and slow reading groups; but it is often difficult to announce grouping assignments without causing some feelings of frustration and unhappiness among those who were included in the least desirable group, and there is usually such a group however the groups are organized. Few people prefer to be cast among the bit players in a play, to be included on the clean-up committee for the party, to be assigned to the second team instead of the varsity. These are not the glamour groups.

Therefore, it is important that teachers create a climate in which pupils understand and accept variability among class members, in which teacher and class explore and use group strengths they discover in this variability, in which group assignments are made and announced with due concern for the sensitivities of class members. The activities that follow suggest procedures you can use to help develop an awareness in your class of the uniqueness of each pupil, and ways of capitalizing on this uniqueness so that disappointments caused by grouping are minimized. Once pupils grasp the idea of variability, they can also accept the possibility of change and growth in themselves. They will learn to accept that skills and abilities they haven't mastered will usually be mastered in time; that the average adult can do anything expected of a school pupil; that while some pupils can read much better than others at eight years of age, all should be able to read adequately before they are eighteen years old. Thus, variability suggests patience.

Understand and accept variability: Many common classroom activities can be used to introduce pupils to the presence of variability in the class. A good example is the weighing and measuring period at the beginning of the year. Construct charts and graphs to visualize differences discovered. Note changes that occur during the year. Often a pupil will go through a growth spurt and pass several pupils who were bigger than he was at the beginning of the year. Use situations such as these to buoy up the spirits of those who feel they will never grow up. Point out to them how they are constantly growing and changing. Boys who are often shorter than girls at ten are usually taller at twenty.

Ask pupils to copy a paragraph you wrote on the board. Display these copies on the bulletin board, arranging them according to various classifications, such as by degree of slant, by style, or by size. Ask pupils to guess who wrote which sample. Discuss reasons for difference in writing style.

An amusing game magnifies family size differences. Ask each pupil to multiply the combined ages of his mother and father by the number of children in his family. This product should be multiplied by the number of uncles and aunts he has. And this product should be multiplied by the number of living grandparents he has. Compare answers—the difference between the highest and lowest answers will be substantial.

An interesting variation of the primary grade Show-and-Tell-Time is called "Surprise." Pupils are paired in random fashion and asked to interview each other. They should compare family backgrounds, interests, special abilities, places where they have lived and traveled, likes and dislikes. Ask them to note similarities and differences. They will usually discover many more differences than similarities. Ask each pair to share some of their discoveries with the rest of the class. Continue with a discussion of the uniqueness of each pupil.

Pose a problem situation that has several possible solutions. Ask pupils to write their solutions to the problem. Read the solutions aloud and discuss the many different approaches to solving the problem the class suggested.

Make an effort to include many activities during the year that permit pupils to discuss and display their ethnic backgrounds. Bring in parents and grandparents who can speak with authority on such topics as family names, national holidays, customs, dress, language, and the like.

Explore and use group strength: [Some pupils can do many things well while others are successful in but few. Constantly probe interests and abilities] Ask pupils to respond to questionnaires that ask them to indicate activities that they enjoy most and those they don't enjoy, and those activities they are successful and unsuccessful doing. Use this information in planning class activities and assignments. Pupils who appear to have few interests and abilities should have many opportunities to develop those they already have, so that they may use the confidence thus gained to develop interests and abilities in other areas. Pupils with wide interests and abilities should be placed into situations where they can explore new dimensions of those interests and abilities, from delving deeper into the subject to teaching other pupils what they already know.

It is often advisable to establish classroom groups on the basis of tasks that require a range of abilities and interests, rather than on the basis of narrow specialties. For example, in unit teaching committees are often organized around specific tasks such as making a mural, setting up a science demonstration, writing a play, and the like. Occasionally, organize committees so that several interest and ability levels of the class are represented on each committee; then assign the same question or problem to each group. Encourage the groups to work independently. It's always interesting to listen to the variety of reports developed from the same basic set of data. Discuss the different ways in which the reports were developed and presented.

One recurring problem involves situations when teams or sides are chosen by the pupils themselves. Some pupils are always chosen last, usually because they are deficient in the skill required in the activity or game. Adapt a procedure long used in bowling leagues. Assign handicap weights to pupils so that the side with poorer players receives a score advantage before the game begins, just as the poorer bowlers on a team are credited with a certain number of knocked down pins before the match begins. Teams that select the poorer players in soft-ball might be credited with an extra run to three runs for each such player selected. In a spelling bee, handicaps might be a certain number of misspelled words not counted for each poor player. The size of the handicap would depend on how bad the player was. As a player improves his skill during the year, his handicap is lowered and finally dropped. But in the meantime, he will have the satisfaction of being selected early like the good players, because he has something to offer to the team that selects him, even if what he offers isn't skill.

Announce groupings considerately: Whether classroom groupings are announced by posting them on the bulletin board or by reading them from a list, it's difficult to mask the disappointment that some pupils feel because they won't be sitting next to their best friend, because they are on a team that has none of the best players, because they will have to work with someone they dislike. It always seemed to me that whenever I would preface an announcement regarding group-ing assignments with a long sermon about the necessity for pupils to work together in many different combinations during the year, that I had more opposition and unhappiness over the groupings I made. Perhaps it was because the pupils sensed I was trying to rationalize some poor combinations I was trying to foist on them, and so they became leery of the whole assignment. Pupils are pretty perceptive about such things. As time went on I didn't talk about my theories of working together before announcing groupings. I waited for a less emotional time to discuss this with them. I merely made the announce-ment with as much confidence as I could muster—as if the decision came from on High. It seemed to work much better, and it did take the spotlight off those "undesirables" who were always the reason for my sermon, try as I might to hide it. If pupils know they will work in many different groups during the year, they will be less apt to react unfavor-ably to being in a group with pupils who are not close to them socially, or who lack the skills required of the group.

IDENTIFY DIFFERENCES WITHIN PUPILS

Variability doesn't only exist *among* pupils in a class. Each pupil also has a combination of contradictions *within himself*. The pupil who is a highly effective leader on the football field may lack much as a leader of a discussion group. The pupil who tackles arithmetic problems with enthusiasm may approach literature classes with disinterest.

It is your responsibility to help pupils see themselves and their potential. As a close and objective observer, you can assess their strengths and weaknesses and show them ways in which they can expand on their strengths and shore up their weaknesses. It is not your responsibility to outline their future life for them, but rather to suggest and guide them to alternative paths they might follow. They will have to make final decisions themselves, but they should arrive at these decisions fully aware of the powers that lie within them.

Pupils' cumulative records should indicate much about the variability within each pupil. During the early weeks of the school year, compare your observations with entries found in pupils' folders. Where discrepancies are noticed, discuss the item frankly with the pupil. Let him know you are interested in him and that you will follow any lead that will help you in your task of assisting him in his search towards an acceptable adult personality.

A little imagination will suggest many simple but informative procedures you can follow to learn more about the interests and strengths of your pupils. For example, suggest that pupils identify written work with a circled 1, 2, or 3 at the bottom. This means: I found this assignment very difficult—I found this assignment challenging but not overly difficult—I found this assignment easy. Also ask them to write a circled A, B, or C after the number. This means: I enjoy this type of assignment very much—I am neutral to this type of assignment —I do not like this type of assignment. This device works particularly well toward the beginning of the year when you are becoming acquainted with your class. It will help you adjust your teaching procedures to the abilities and interests of your class.

As the school year unfolds, pupils with marked differences in ability and interest in different areas often ask if they can oblige themselves to exceptionally high standards in a favored area in return for lesser requirements in others. Surprisingly, this will often result in better work in both areas if you handle it right. It's a matter of giving a pupil enough rope. Once he has demonstrated to himself and to you how good his work can be in one area, the struggle to set higher standards in other areas is half won. Variability within a person doesn't necessarily mean positive and negative values. It can also mean varying levels of excellence. Work toward that goal with your pupils.

A good testing program will help pupils understand their own variability if handled properly. While you may not want to give out achievement and intelligence test scores to pupils, you should discuss their results with them in general terms. Help each pupil analyze strengths and weaknesses, and develop plans for improvement where it is in order and where it is possible.

Teacher-made tests, if constructed imaginatively, can lead to interesting class discussions on pupil variability. Some pupils insist they do better on objective test items than they do on essay test items, or vice versa. Ask pupils to respond to several true/false or multiple choice items. Then ask them to respond to an essay question that is based on an interpretation of the objective items they just answered. Pupils who get the objective items correct and the essay question wrong should be led to see that their knowledge of individual facts doesn't mean much unless they can draw them together into correct generalizations. Pupils who write an acceptable answer to the essay question, but miss many of the objective items, should be led to see that if they draw a generalization without a clear understanding of the supporting data, their understanding of the generalization is weak.

Various sociometric and personality tests are also available to teachers who want to help pupils gain a clearer perspective of themselves. These testing devices are valuable if you understand them thoroughly, and if your pupils clearly understand that the tests are used to help pupils in their most interesting school search, that of learning to know themselves.

ADJUST ACTIVITIES TO THE INDIVIDUAL

The individual pupil often becomes lost in a welter of statistics. When we grade tests and assignments, we use various measures of central tendency to discover where the scores tended to bunch up, that is to discover how well the average pupil did. And we also use various measures of variability to discover how far some of the scores deviated from this average, that is, to discover what the non-average pupil did. We end up with three groups of pupils: the large group who did average work, and the smaller groups who did better and worse than average. All pupils are placed in one or another category and so each individual effort on a group test or assignment winds up a small part of a group comparative evaluation.

One way to change the emphasis from group comparative evaluations to individual evaluations is to ask pupils to estimate their ability to do the work before they begin. Ask them to survey the work required, and then to indicate at the top of their paper or on a separate piece of paper they keep how much of the test or assignment they think they can complete, and the grade they think they will get on their work. This will make them think in terms of an individual goal in which they will compete with their own estimate of their ability. They may reach their goal, they may come short of it, or they may exceed it. In any case, your evaluation of their work will appear to them to be more oriented to them individually than to the entire group.

Counsel with pupils who typically show an inability to correctly assess their ability to carry out a task. Help them see each school task as an individual assignment, even if it is given to an entire class. Use an analogy from the building trade. When a building is scheduled to be constructed, several contractors are invited to submit bids. While each contractor has the same assignment and works with the same basic set of data, each must make an estimate of the job that is consistent with his ability to carry out the task successfully and within the financial limits of his bid. Contractors who are successful are contractors who can best estimate their ability to do the job they bid on, and who can carry out the assignment most efficiently.

Procedures that require pupils to consider school tasks in individual terms can do much to lessen the problems that arise when you adjust assignments so that the pupils are given assignments commensurate with their ability. Unless the idea of varying capabilities is properly handled, resentment can arise within the class. Some of the average and better pupils may deliberately do poor work so that their assignments are also reduced. Some of the less able pupils may be subjected to the resentment of their fellow pupils because less is required of them.

By placing a greater emphasis on pupils competing with themselves rather than with other members of the class, you will develop an atmosphere in which pupils will show less concern for the amount of work they *must* do and more concern for the amount they *can* do. Several times during the year, ask pupils to write short essays in which they assess themselves as students. Ask them to write specifically of strengths and weaknesses they have and of their efforts to build and improve on these. Save these papers so that they can re-read what they wrote earlier in the year. Challenge them to get as close to their potential during the year as they can. Encourage them to consider themselves as contractors who are moving up from bidding on garages to bidding on skyscrapers.

While much of the activity pupils engage in during the year is group-oriented, pupils ought to have several opportunities to escape from mass assignments, mass presentations, and mass tests. They ought to do something on their own. A pupil ought to work at least once on a significant project of his own that is tailored to his unique interests and abilities. He ought to have a chance to show what he can do on a project that no other pupil has in common with him.

One way of doing this is to free each pupil for an entire week to carry out a private project or investigation. During this week, he would not be required to participate in the regular activities of the class. He would concentrate his energies on his own project and report.

Begin sometime late September or early October when pupils have become familiar with the routine of the room, and when there are enough weeks remaining in the school year so that each pupil can have a week of his own. Meet with each pupil during the week or weeks preceding the week he is scheduled to carry out his investigation. During these preliminary meetings help him identify and outline his investigation. Topics will vary in scope and complexity depending on the interests and ability of the pupil involved. Pupils will often select topics that deal with the history of their town or region, with occupations, with science, with biography, with political issues. Creative pupils might spend the week composing a song, writing a story or play, or making an extensive model of something. Allow considerable freedom in selecting topics as long as the pupil's proposal indicates he is approaching his task seriously.

Each pupil should begin his formal work on Monday. If possible, set up a semi-private place in the room for him to use during the week.

While a pupil will probably want to participate in some class activities, he will also want to work on his project undisturbed while the rest of the class is engaged in activities that might disturb him. He should be relatively free to work in the school library and interview school personnel who could be of help to him. Most pupils will also spend a considerable amount of time on their project during the after school and evening hours. Be available for help and encouragement if a pupil seeks your counsel, but don't develop his report for him. It should be his alone if he is to profit from the experience.

The project should be so organized that he can give a rather extensive report to the class sometime Friday afternoon. Encourage pupils to be imaginative in reporting their findings, and to use such devices as bulletin boards, tape recorders, overhead projectors, dioramas, and puppetry. As the year unfolds, these reports will become a high point of each week. Pupils rarely have such an opportunity to spend so much time investigating a subject they are interested in. Experience has shown that most pupils rise to the challenge this activity presents and do as good a job as they are capable of doing. Those who don't should return to their normal class life and routine just as soon as they show that they are not devoting their attention to their project.

Since these reports come a week apart and cover such a wide variety of topics, each report will be judged on its own merits by pupils. There is relatively little effort to compare reports with the ones that were given earlier. By and large, pupils seem more interested in enjoying the reports than in evaluating them. But the pupil who gave the report is always keenly interested in your evaluation of his report. The half hour the two of you will spend after school that day discussing the report may well be the most important half hour of his year.

DON'T FORGET ABILITY EXTREMES

At the present time the unique needs of most gifted and slow learning pupils in our country must be met in normal classrooms if they are to be met. Unless your school system places such pupils in special classes you can usually expect from two to four of each extreme in your classroom. These pupils can actually add much to the total experience and learning of the group, but you must organize class activities to take advantage of what they need and what they have to offer.

Gifted pupils: Definitions of gifted pupils vary but most authortiies agree that gifted pupils have a strong potential for productive and evaluative thinking. They are usually quite adept at problem solving; they suggest innovations; and properly motivated, they can serve as excellent catalysts in class discussion. These factors suggest that gifted pupils can do much to enrich the learning of the entire class. The speed at which they normally master skills gives them the time to follow their curiosity and discover and report on side issues that will interest and inform their classmates. The following suggestions illustrate the type of activities you might consider.

Gifted pupils will often learn the four arithmetic operations more rapidly than the rest of the class. Suggest they develop games that will help their classmates learn these skills. They may be able to devise short-cuts to obtain answers to more complex problems quickly. They might want to investigate and report on other methods of working problems such as the Egyptian and Gelosia methods of multiplication. They may enjoy making simple computing devices such as Napier's Bones. Most books on arithmetic puzzles and tricks will describe these and many other fascinating approaches to arithmetic computation.

Gifted pupils can frequently carry out high quality individual research projects in science and social studies units. They are particularly adept at doing creative work, and work that requires the study and interpretation of interrelationships. For example, such a pupil could study a leading industry in the community. He could trace the raw products used back to their source and the finished manufactured product to its ultimate consumers. He could relate the two and the economic significance of each in the communities where the industry has an impact.

Assign gifted pupils to different groups during the year as pupils work together in smaller groups. These pupils have the ability to encourage effective group effort. They can ask the right questions and suggest hypotheses when the group is seeking answers to questions. Through this, they can demonstrate critical thinking to their classmates in a way that you could never match because you cannot become a member of such groups. While gifted pupils occasionally become uninterested in such group investigations since they already "know the answer," they can still serve effectively if you can interest them in the interplay of group work. Challenge them to concentrate their efforts on the group itself rather than on the specific task the group is trying to solve. These pupils often assume managerial positions in adult life so they need many opportunities to work with others effectively in situations where they are the most knowledgeable person in the group.

Slow learners: Slow learners learn to read later than the rest of the class and their annual achievement in all areas is generally less than what normal children accomplish during a year. Since curricular materials and instruction in the typical classroom are geared to the normal pupil, slow learners fall farther and farther behind their class-mates as the years progress. They become frustrated by constant failure and frequently express this frustration through some form of deviant behavior.

These pupils need large portions of love and patient understanding. Many come from home environments that accentuate their learning problems. You may have to assume some responsibilities in teaching these pupils that parents assume in most homes. One major problem you will face is that of finding enough time to work with these pupils. They require more individual attention than the normal pupil, and their attention span to a specific task is often limited. The suggestions below illustrate the type of activities you can carry out that will deal with the several concerns raised above.

It is important that slow learners develop good work habits and the ability to work independently. These skills will permit them to make maximum use of the limited knowledge and ability they have. One procedure takes but a few additional moments when you make your plans for the next school day. Determine how you will adjust assignments for your slow learning pupils and then write out the day's assignments on a slip of paper for each of these pupils so that he can see at a glance what will be expected of him that day. Use a little imagination and humor as you adjust assignments. You might ask a pupil to do such things as learn the spelling words in the list that begin with the letters in his name, to work the five arithmetic problems that look the easiest and try to do the one that looks the hardest, to read the story assigned in reading and then see if he can stump you with a riddle based on his reading. Assignments such as these can do much to encourage the slow learner to work to his capacity because they remove him from competition with his classmates, and they buoy up his confidence because he knows you went to a little extra trouble to adjust the class assignment to his particular needs.

Set aside the first few minutes of work and study periods to work with your slow pupils. During this period the rest of the class will be most occupied and you will have fewer distractions. Also slow learning pupils will profit most from instruction given them just prior to independent work.

Individual flash cards can be a big help to slow learning pupils. They permit such pupils to work at skills in odd moments, alone or with others. Encourage pupils to develop their own flash cards as needed from a pile of blank cards readily available. Help them devise interesting and challenging games with their cards. You might even have a "mortgage burning" ceremony every Friday afternoon for cards no longer needed.

Concentrate instruction on things that are of practical value to them whenever possible. For example, slow learners should understand local and regional problems even if they have a lesser understanding of national and international problems. They should understand electricity as it affects them in household appliances even if they don't understand its theoretical foundations. They should know how to work effectively with money, time, and measurement. And they should know how to read and follow directions even if they find it difficult to appreciate great literature.

Slow learners frequently have social problems. Lack of confidence and poorly developed oral communication skills accent this. Develop their confidence in themselves by placing them into social situations where their success is assured. Ask them to help you whenever possible to give them a feeling of personal worth. Encourage them to achieve acceptance through generally accepted behavior patterns rather than through deviant behavior by rewarding good behavior and by ignoring attempts for attention through deviant behavior. The slow learner who works in a pressure-free classroom is most apt to work to his potential and achieve satisfaction from that.

ASSIST THE CULTURALLY DISADVANTAGED PUPIL

The gap between the simple life of yesteryear and the complex life of tomorrow has particular significance for one segment of our school population who have come to be identified as the culturally disadvantaged. These pupils come from homes in which parents have received a limited education, are not personally committed to the kinds of learning fostered in the schools, and often work at low paying laboring jobs that may be obsolete by the time their children grow up. Many of these families are on relief. Many of these children are being reared by a single parent. They bear the brunt of their parent's unsuccessful adulthood.

These pupils can look forward in a few years to an adult life in which intellectual ability and technical skill will be required of practically all who would work for a living. In addition, automation and other industrial advances will permit workers to earn a living in fewer hours than are required now. Workers of the future will have much more leisure time available to them. Culturally disadvantaged children are not ready to cope with either of these developments; and their parents lack the background, and often the interest, to assist them. Our nation cannot afford to support these children through their adult life. But if they are to be prepared to face the adult world as normal producing citizens, the schools must assume a large share of the responsibility of preparing them.

It's probably safe to say that most teachers have a few disadvantaged children in their classes. Some teachers work with an entire class of such children. Because the problem is becoming increasingly acute in some areas, extensive programs have been set up to deal with the challenges these children offer.

The individual teacher can offer these children one important thing that large foundations and crash programs and bureaucratic school machinery can never offer directly though. The individual teacher can be a concrete example of all the abstract theory that has been developed about meeting the needs of these pupils.

You can become one adult in these pupils' lives who can show them a life most cannot see in their homes or in their communities. You can show them what a successful adult "looks like." Let them become acquainted with an adult who can cope with the world today, and who will cope with whatever the world of tomorrow will bring, an adult who is committed to values that will not change regardless of what the future might bring. Show them an adult who is dedicated to fulfilling his responsibilities, who is honest in his dealings with his colleagues and pupils, who has a sense of right and wrong in any situation he faces, and who acts accordingly.

Be optimistic about life in your dealings with these pupils. They have known little but defeat. Leave your petty problems home—they can top any you have. Show them an adult to emulate; they have known too many of the other kind. They will respect those things the school believes in when they respect their teachers, who represent the school.

The typical elementary textbook assumes an experience level above that of many culturally deprived pupils. Therefore, you will be forced to supplement textbook material if you teach such pupils, particularly in reading and arithmetic.

The experience chart in its various forms is still the best single device to use in such situations. Primary teachers can develop reading charts from the backgrounds their pupils bring to school, whether that be littered alleys, rural shanties, or up-hollow cabins. Once developed, these charts can be used over and over again as pupils learn to read and discover that writing is a means of recording what they know and have experienced. Don't seek out the sordid in their meager lives. Rather, concentrate on whatever islands of beauty they can discover.

Since older pupils may reject large charts as childish, you might change the format somewhat. Develop stories initially on the chalkboard. Ask a pupil to copy the story before it is erased. Reproduce the stories on ditto masters and run off enough copies for your class. Then use this material in your teaching where it is appropriate. Pupils can assemble the pages thus developed into a booklet that will grow in size and value through the year.

Sharpen your storytelling ability if you teach culturally deprived pupils. Few children can resist a good story, so enrich your pupils' knowledge of the outside world by telling them about it in as graphic and interesting a way as you can. You alone in their lives can enlarge their horizons. When you have told a story, develop a chart from it so they can read about it again later and recall the experience they had hearing it.

Arithmetic is often the bane of these pupils because their constricted world does not include abstractions, and we have a tendency to be abstract when we teach arithmetic. Make arithmetic concrete for such pupils, even if this means that you ask them to determine which of two alleys contains more empty bottles for want of something better. Man makes decisions on the basis of his interpretation of quantitative data. The decision to clean up litter in alleys is made on the basis of the amount of litter present, and on the effort necessary to clean it up.

Instead of asking pupils to work story problems that don't relate to their lives, ask pupils to develop word problems from number problems you give them. Suggest that they draw their word problems from their recent experience. Through such activities they can be led to realize that $4 + 3$ isn't necessarily an abstraction, but rather something that occurs to many people in many different circumstances every day.

All arithmetic can be defined as an attempt to equalize two sides of an equation, to find a numeral on one side of the equation that matches in value the combination of data gathered on the other side of the equation. This is an exciting search. In a larger sense it permits civilization as we know it to exist. Such conceptions as a favorable trade balance, conservation, and equality of opportunity are allied to it. These pupils have not discovered in their lives how to equalize the equation. They haven't discovered the combination that will permit them to make effective use of what the world has to offer them.

Teachers often become so concerned that pupils acquire basic skills, which give substance to life, that they neglect the arts, which give meaning to life. Disadvantaged pupils are often so seriously deficient in basic school skills that there is a great temptation to spend as much time as possible working on basic language and number skills with these pupils, to the detriment of work in the arts. These pupils have as much or more need to develop an understanding and love for music and art and literature. The arts feed the spirit, and they are available to any who want to draw sustenance from them, regardless of financial or social circumstances.

Because of this, part of your program to develop understanding and appreciation of the arts should seem to flow out of everyday living. For example, select recordings of several musical works you want to acquaint your class with during the year. You will probably be most successful with works having strong melodic themes. Introduce these selections casually as background music during study periods, during the half hour before school begins, as pupils come in from recess, during activity periods, etc. Say little about the music—let it speak for itself. Identify the selection being played with a notation on the board. One day you will hear someone whistle or hum a selection from one of the works. Then you will know it's time to introduce your class to the composer, to the themes that make up the work, and to other information that will increase their appreciation of the work. Do this informally. You don't have to force good music or art or literature on pupils. The works will sell themselves.

Selections will vary from year to year and from teacher to teacher. If you capitalize on the many opportunities you have during the year to play parts or all of the works you selected, you will discover that most of your pupils will know the works by the end of the year; and more important, they will have developed a real appreciation for at least a few. The following is a selection of musical works I used one year with a sixth grade class.

J. S. Bach:	Toccata and Fugue in D Minor
Beethoven:	Sixth Symphony
Franck:	D Minor Symphony
Mozart:	Jupiter Symphony
Handel:	Water Music Suite
Gershwin:	Rhapsody in Blue
Copland:	Appalachian Spring
Debussy:	Afternoon of a Faun

Follow the same procedure with art works. It's not difficult to borrow good art reproductions from your local library if you live in a city. Most colleges have good art collections they are willing to lend to responsible teachers who seriously pursue a program of art appreciation with their pupils. Set up a small gallery along part of a wall. Display several pictures at a time. Change them every few weeks, but bring back favorites from time to time.

Spend some time each day reading to your class. Select good fiction and non-fiction books that will give your pupils something to aim for in their own future reading. Study the books carefully before reading them to your class so that you can interpret the story through your delivery. And then constantly work to improve your delivery. If pupils look forward to listening to good books being read to them for fifteen minutes a day, they will be much more inclined to want to read good books themselves. In selecting books remember that a person's listening vocabulary is larger than his reading vocabulary, so you don't have to limit yourself to books written for young readers. A good many adult books are excellent to read to pupils.

DEAL INTELLIGENTLY AND COMPASSIONATELY WITH SPECIAL PROBLEMS

You can expect that several emotionally difficult situations will occur during the school year. Events such as a serious sickness or death in a pupil's family, the loss of a job, or a separation or divorce can drain much of the vitality from the pupils directly involved. On these occasions, teachers have a responsibility to help these pupils in any way that befits the situation. It's completely inexcusable for a teacher to slip up on such a responsibility.

It doesn't take much time or energy to visit a parent who is seriously ill in the hospital. Let him know that his child is concerned about the illness, and that you are doing what you can to help the child through this difficult period. Most parents will worry about their children when they are sick and away from them for an extended period. A short and reassuring visit from one of their children's teachers would be especially appreciated.

A more common practice is that of a class sending cards and letters to a classmate who is at home or in the hospital with an extended illness. Write fairly frequently instead of sending a whole box full of letters once or twice. Set up a mail box in the classroom, or organize the class so that several pupils write each day or so. Keep the missing pupil informed about things the class is doing during his absence. As he approaches the end of his convalescence, begin to bring him up-to-date on the schoolwork he has missed so that he can rejoin his classes with a minimum of trouble. Make several personal visits.

A death in the family can be a very shattering event to a pupil, or it can be received with relative calm. It depends on the age of the pupil, the emotional ties between the pupil and the deceased, the circumstances surrounding the death, and the religious beliefs of the pupil. Remove the pupil from his classmates before he is told of the death. It's better to have someone in his family tell him; but if you have to do it, you should also drive him home. At such a time, the fewer people involved, the better. Tell your classes about the death after the pupil has gone home; and suggest they take their cue from him when he returns. If he still appears deeply saddened upon his return, the class should make every effort to show compassion in their class and playground behavior. If it appears that he has made a satisfactory adjustment to his new situation in life, then they should allow him to pick up where he left off. Beyond expressions of sympathy, you and his classmates should refrain from asking questions or raising the subject. If he wants to talk about it, let him take the initiative.

A separation or divorce can also be accepted differently by different pupils. In some circumstances, it might be a relief. In others, it could be a completely shattering event. The pupil whose parents' marriage breaks up doesn't usually have an opportunity to stay away from school for a few days while he re-builds his world, like the pupil who has a death in the family. It's not proper to discuss a divorce with the class. If the pupil wants to tell his friends about it, let him do it—but you shouldn't. You can be very helpful during such a period, though, by being a sympathetic listener if he wants to talk about it. Your contributions to the discussion should reassure him that his parents are both fine people who were very fond of each other at one time, but who ran into personal problems they were unable to solve. Even if one (or both) of his parents are worthless, it's not your business to tell him.

You will usually have at least one physically handicapped pupil in your room. Handicapped people don't want pity. They just want a chance to show they are human beings and not freaks. They want an opportunity to discover what they can do with what they have. Give them a chance to become independent of others as much as possible. They will repay you a thousandfold by teaching you lessons in courage and determination. They will have a positive impact on the entire class.

Our nine year old son can tie his shoe strings, and he plays catcher on his first place Little League baseball team. There's nothing remarkable about that except that he was born with only one hand. He's much better off for having learned to take care of himself than he would have been had he been allowed to become dependent on others to help him with activities that normally take two hands.

Help handicapped pupils when you must so they won't become completely frustrated. Adjust school activities when you must so they won't be embarrassed or attract undue attention. But always accept them for what they are; pupils who are normal except for one or two of the many functions of the human body.

Classmates can be kind or cruel to handicapped and emotionally saddened pupils, often unwittingly. If you don't make a big to-do over such pupils and draw attention to them, neither will the others. They will be more apt to accept them for what they are. They will play and argue and fight and make up with them. But they'll also give such pupils a chance to adjust normally to the world they'll have to live in, a world of dreams and shattered dreams, of successes and failures, of happiness and sadness.

6

ACCENT WITH
LIGHT MOMENTS

DEVELOP A SENSE OF HUMOR

Light moments add sparkle and life to any classroom. They provide a positive outlet for tensions that develop in any group, and so they permit the group to weld and work together more effectively. Seek out these moments and capitalize on them when they occur.

Your success in seizing upon such moments will depend, to an extent, on your sense of humor. Researchers studying teacher effectiveness have continually found that a sense of humor ranks high in the personality composition of successful teachers. A sense of humor is a rather elusive thing, composed of many elements. The following three seem to have particular relevance for classroom teaching, though. Concentrate on them as you continue to develop your own sense of humor as a teacher.

Show yourself a part of the older generation, but also apart from it. The traditional stereotype of teachers places us somewhat in the character class. Pupils delight in this stereotype just as we did a generation back. It won't hurt you to play along with it from time to time. Let your pupils pull a prank on you occasionally. It will brighten and lighten their day a bit and enrich their remembrance of you. But while pupils enjoy assuming that we are antiquated enough to give them firsthand information on the Spanish-American War, they also appreciate our willingness to cross over the desk periodically and demonstrate that we can see the next generation's point of view and are sympathetic with it. To young pupils, a teacher with a sense of humor is an adult with enough of the pixie about him to move easily and willingly between the worlds of the present and next generations.

Take teaching seriously, but don't take yourself too seriously. Pupils react positively to teachers who take their professions seriously and show it in the preparation and caliber of their work. But they react negatively to teachers who identify themselves so closely with the seriousness of their work that they make themselves unapproachable on an informal basis. Relax with your class. Be willing to talk of the fables and foibles of adult life. Laugh with them at all that is pompous, false, self-seeking, or intolerant. These are things that must be laughed at if our society is to improve, and only a teacher who can see and admit these things in himself and in his generation can teach his pupils to resist them whenever they occur.

Find humor in classroom activities, but don't force it in. Most of us can remember two types of humorous teachers. The first arranged his presentations so that he could use the stock of jokes he had been telling for years. We laughed but we weren't always amused. The second drew his humor spontaneously out of classroom life. Much of his humor wasn't funny when we repeated it to others later, but it was funny when we heard it. The second type of teacher recognized that humor is basically an accenting of incongruency in life. He called attention to school incongruencies and magnified them. Thus, he drew humor out of an arithmetic error his class caught him at, or out of a study period disrupted by noisy jackhammers on the street outside the classroom. Use good humorous stories in your teaching when they fit, but try to draw much of your classroom humor out of the everyday happenings that occur in your room.

Humor can become a normal part of class life in other ways too. Most teachers read to their classes. As you select material to read, don't forget to introduce your class to humor that is found in literature, from satire to tall tales to sheer nonsense. It forms a delightful page in literature they should get to know.

Help your class develop an appreciation of cartoon humor by

displaying good cartoons selected from magazines and newspapers. Your pupils will help you expand your collection. Mount the best cartoons on cardboard and file them by topics for future use. As you build your collection, display cartoons so that they correlate with current class activities. You can also mask cartoon captions and ask pupils to write captions that fit the drawings. Cut news photographs from the daily papers and ask pupils to write humorous captions for them. Display and study political and editorial cartoons. Show pupils how such artists use humor to express their point of view effectively.

It's not uncommon to have a pupil in your class who torments fellow pupils with pointed and often cruel jests. His quick wit usually draws enough response to encourage him to further jokes directed toward classmates. Deal individually with such pupils. Intelligent as they are, they are often so caught up with themselves that they are unaware that they are progressively antagonizing their fellow pupils. Involve them in positive programs that will use the real ability they frequently have to construct humorous situations. Ask them to write skits and plays and to contribute to the school paper. Encourage them to read library books written by great humorists. Many of these pupils can be guided into cartoon humor once they discover the caption is often as important as the drawing.

Many adults tell humorous stories and jokes poorly. Begin to develop storytelling skills in young people by including joke telling in show-and-tell periods. Encourage pupils to remember and relate good jokes they hear. Discuss jokes and the proper delivery of jokes with your class. Stress the importance of relating each part of the joke to the punch line, of telling the story in proper sequence, of using dialog effectively, of inflecting the voice properly, and of telling jokes and stories with a straight face.

CELEBRATE SPECIAL DAYS AND EVENTS

Anniversaries mean enough to most people so that they relax their normal way of living somewhat on the day the anniversary occurs. Special traditions develop around major observances and many of these carry over into school life. Birthdays, and religious and national celebrations comprise most such special days observed during the year. Each has special implications for classroom commemoration.

Birthdays: Birthday celebrations differ from other special days in that they focus on an individual pupil. This is one of the more pleasant aspects of classroom birthday observances. It's good for a pupil to be the center of attention once in a while.

Let primary grade pupils construct paper hats or crowns to wear on their birthdays. Let these pupils become your teacher's helper that day and select the games and lead the exercises. In some schools the birthday child brings a treat, usually candy, for the other pupils in the class. Consider varying this by asking the pupil to make or give something to the entire class as a group, such as a special bulletin board display, a one-man puppet show, a puzzle for them to figure out, an amusing film or filmstrip (ordered from your school district's collection), a new game, or a bouquet of flowers.

Normally, though, the birthday child receives the gifts. Suggest that pupils make birthday presents for their classmates with the only stipulation that they can't spend more than a nickel for materials. Thus, a hand-made book jacket, a smooth stone to carry in the pocket, a poem written for the occasion, a shoe shine, a pencil holder, a hair ribbon, or a puzzle made especially for the birthday child all will serve to make the day more joyful and memorable. This activity and the one preceding it teach pupils that the thought and imagination given to a gift are much more important than the amount of money spent on it.

Some pupils have birthdays over the weekend or during vacations. Weekend birthdays can be celebrated on Friday or Monday, but vacation birthdays are another matter. Get together with such pupils and select a date during the school year when no one else has a birthday. Fete these people on that date with special activities.

Practically every day of the year is the anniversary of some famous person. Encyclopedias, almanacs, and school calendars give a comprehensive listing of such dates. Ask pupils to look up the story of a famous person who was born on the same day they were and report on it to the class on their birthday. If the person is still living, suggest that the pupil make and send him a birthday card.

Ask pupils to select a child born in the community on their birthday and write his parents a letter of congratulation. Names can be found in newspaper accounts and hospital records.

Religious observances: It's rather difficult to ignore the major religious festivals, although they do give pause to teachers who work with pupils of several faiths and/or pupils with no religious convictions. On the other hand, good teachers do not ignore important aspects of our culture just because they are difficult to handle in a classroom. They discuss elections, civil rights, urban renewal, fluoridation, and many other controversial issues. They also recognize the existence of Christmas, the Passover, Easter, and other major religious festivals for what they are; religious festivals, and not primarily days for reindeer and bunnies.

While public school teachers should not teach religion, they do have an obligation to teach *about* religion, about the history and customs of religious movements that affect the lives of their pupils. The topic will most frequently arise in connection with social studies activities, and during the observance of major religious festivals. Your pupils can often assist by telling the class about their churches and the major festivals their churches observe. They can answer questions their classmates raise. They can seek answers to questions they can't answer from their parents and from their religious leaders. Classroom discussions should not dwell on doctrinal differences except in a purely explanatory way. Most youngsters lack the background to engage profitably in such discussion, and only rarely will such discussion be proper in a public school classroom. Strike a note for tolerant inquiry in your class. Religious convictions spring from deep within the heart of members of a faith. Such convictions should not be treated as objects of derision and laughter.

Most major religious festivals have developed a secular tradition around them, however, and much school observance of these days will of necessity revolve around these secular themes. Look in encyclopedias and holiday books for traditions developed in other lands and introduce them to your pupils during the days and weeks preceding the holiday. Seek the history behind the traditions we observe and tell your class about them. Read to your class selections from the great literature that has developed around these festivals.

National and patriotic observances: In recent years we have somehow gotten away from recalling famous days. It's a shame. Many teachers might be encouraged to spend a few minutes talking about phonographs on February 19 if they knew that Edison patented the phonograph on that date in 1878, but they don't know it and their pupils are the worse for it.

Use encyclopedias and almanacs to discover interesting and important events that occur each month. Construct a bulletin board display that will accent several such events each month. Weave these events into your classroom activities and studies during that month. Encourage pupils to use these events in writing assignments during the month. Perhaps a committee of pupils could even select the events to commemorate and construct the bulletin board display.

Days that have special patriotic significance should be observed with special ceremonies, planned and directed by a class committee. These ceremonies could include patriotic songs, a short talk or skit about the occasion, and a flag salute or drill.

Construct your own flags and banners. Art guides and books give directions for stitchery work. Encourage pupils to design and make banners stitched on burlap that could be hung in the room during periods of patriotic and national observance, such as a presidential anniversary, an election week, city and state anniversary weeks, and other events deemed important by the class. Let your pupils carry the current banner before them on a standard as they march to the cafeteria and playground. Design the banners so they are general in theme. For example, one banner could cover all presidential anniversaries. Five or six such banners constructed early in the school year should serve all events observed during the school year.

Turn one wall into a room calendar. Assign a day of the month to each pupil and ask him to depict that day artistically on a sheet of construction paper. When his day arrives he should affix his paper to the wall on the spot it would normally occupy on a calendar. The pupil may choose to commemorate some historical event that occurred on that date or some event that occurred in the community or classroom that day. At the end of the month, pupils will have a visual reminder of the month.

Older pupils may enjoy discussing the idea of anniversaries. They will have celebrated quite a few without ever really stopping to think why people observe anniversaries. Discuss such questions as: Why are anniversaries observed annually instead of semi-annually or biannually? Why have vacations become an important part of many anniversary celebrations? Why do people entertain more during such holiday seasons? Why do we observe some anniversaries, such as Washington's birthday and Christmas, and not others such as Wilson's birthday and Epiphany? Why does eating play an important part in many anniversary celebrations? Such a discussion may not immediately answer the questions raised, but it will introduce pupils to thoughts about anniversaries that probably hadn't occurred to them before.

PLAN GOOD PARTIES

Parties give you an excellent opportunity to develop social graces and skills in pupils. Let your class give enough parties during the year so that everyone will have an opportunity to help plan at least one party.

Schools traditionally schedule Halloween, Christmas, and Valentine parties. These three occasions have become such a part of our life, though, that they have lost much of their effectiveness as vehicles for training pupils in party-giving skills. Even experienced, imaginative adult partygivers have trouble varying the recipe for these parties. Why not let your class develop their imagination and ability on such occasions as the first day of fall, winter, and spring, or Hans Christian Andersen's birthday (April 2), or the middle day of the school year, or the anniversary of the patenting of the phonograph, or even the mayor's birthday? At the beginning of the year list twenty or so intriguing party possibilities and ask your class to select five or six. Each pupil should sign up for one of the parties. It's advisable to limit committee membership to five since this will permit all members to participate actively in discussions, decisions, and direction of the party.

Ask party committees to begin their work shortly after the conclusion of the preceding party. Each member should have a specific responsibility. The chairman should coordinate the efforts of the group and conduct committee meetings. The invitations chairman should get the class interested in the party. Puzzles, riddles, posters, and bulletin board displays can do much to develop anticipation in the class and prepare them for the party. The decorations chairman should plan and supervise the construction and placement of decorations for the party.

Decorations can do much to establish the party theme in the minds of the participants. There is no reason why they can't often be put up several days before the party as Christmas trees and Valentine boxes are. The program chairman should suggest activities and the sequence of activities. He should also serve as master of ceremonies or game leader during the party. Generally, it's better to have one person direct the party than to have the entire committee share direction. The refreshments chairman should plan and serve a menu that fits the theme of the party. The entire committee should discuss and agree on plans, but individual members should be responsible for executing specific assignments.

Consider also short informal parties in connection with social studies and science units. For example, a unit on Mexico could culminate with a noon meal in a nearby Mexican cafe instead of at the school cafeteria. Most such specialty restaurants are happy to arrange inexpensive meals for potential future customers, especially if the meal can be served after the peak lunch hour. You might also consider preparing such a meal in the classroom. Pupils will learn much from actually working with the ingredients used in cooking the meal. Properly approached, many school cooks are willing to work with responsible pupils on such projects as baking bread or rolls in connection with a unit on grains or on the chemistry of cooking.

Invite your class in small groups to your house during the year. Perhaps a group planning a special presentation for the PTA could have one of their planning sessions at your house one evening. Or you might invite a group over to make and decorate a cookie house that could be displayed in the classroom during December and eaten the day before Christmas vacation. Invite the library assistants or the patrol boys over one evening. Arrange it so that each pupil in your room is invited to one of these informal sessions during the year. Show them gracious entertaining on cokes and cookies.

What should you teach your pupils about entertaining through the parties your class gives during the year?

A good party has an imaginative twist to it. Most people react favorably to imaginative party themes that are effectively carried out through decorations and activities. In seeking an imaginative twist suggest that pupils study the physical facilities available, the group, and the purpose of the party. Thus, a class with a predominance of boys might decide to accent the comic side of Valentine's Day at their party; or a class with a member who lives next door to the school might construct and operate a spook-house in his basement for the Halloween enjoyment of other classes. Unusual party treatments are worth the effort it takes to develop them because they add a note of anticipation that puts everyone in a party mood.

A good party is well planned. Attention to details, important in any undertaking, is crucial to the success of most parties. Teach pupils to plan for calamities that might befall their parties. For example, extra equipment should be on hand for games requiring special equipment that can break. Suggest that they plan more activities than time will allow so that unsuccessful activities can be cut short. Cater to boys' likes and dislikes if necessary since girls are more willing to play "boy" games than boys are willing to play "girl" games. Alternate active games with quiet games. Schedule activities so that participants end one activity in a position that will permit the start of the next activity without a lot of movement. Keep directions and rules short and simple, and demonstrate whenever possible. Stop playing a game while the group is still enjoying it and they'll want to play it again sometime. Plan food lines so that pupils with food don't have to pass those still waiting. Don't serve foods that accent the clean-up problem.

A good party encourages conversation. Most party activities should stimulate conversation. Ice-breakers introduce strangers, active games break down inhibitions, mental games stimulate the intellect, refreshments permit an extended period of pleasant conversation. Teach pupils to consider these factors as they plan activities. Thus, ice-breakers serve a much more useful function at parties early in the school year than they do in May. A successful party is so paced that participants have opportunities for brief conversations during the directed activities. These brief conversations often determine the grouping that develops during the unstructured refreshment period. Arrange seating at parties so that people can sit in small groups. Some successful party givers even suggest that there should be fewer chairs than people to force people to move around.

Suggestions such as the foregoing, known and followed by experienced hosts and hostesses, must be learned sometime by everyone. Since parties are a part of school life, use these opportunities to teach principles and skills of successful entertaining.

ENJOY PLAY PERIODS

The relatively unstructured play periods before and after school, and during recess and noon hour can be considered laboratory periods in human relations. Pupils should have opportunities to try out ways of getting along together that they have discussed in school. The presence of pupils from other rooms on the same playground may complicate things somewhat, but it's good for pupils to learn to share facilities and activities.

Some problems can be avoided through sensible scheduling of play areas and equipment. The most commonly used procedure, that of awarding the play area or equipment to the first person or group who claims it, does little more than encourage frantic foot races down the corridors and inevitable fights among opposing groups who always seem to arrive in a dead heat. It's better to work out a sign-up and assignment procedure such as the one described below.

Each class sharing facilities during the same time period should elect a boy and girl to represent them on a playground committee that meets each Thursday after school. The committee and their advisor should consider the season, the weather, current interests of pupils, and specific requests, and then assign areas to activities. Thus, a concrete area might become a skating rink one week and a hop-scotch area the next. The tether balls may be assigned to a class sponsoring a room tether ball tournament for two days and left open the other three days. The north half of the playground may be assigned to flag football, and the south half may be assigned to several activities such as dodge ball, kick goal, freeze tag, races, and soccer on successive days. Groups with specific requests should send their requests through their room representatives. Always leave several play areas open for pupils who want to do something different.

Distribute copies of the committee's assignments to each room on Friday. Establish ground rules for activities whenever this appears advisable. For example,

> Flag football teams will be chosen from among those present at
> 8:30 in the morning. The same sides will remain in effect all day.
> (16).

The (16) refers to the minimum number of participants that must be
present to hold the area for that activity that day. If fewer are present,
the teacher on duty can cut their playing area or else permit a different
game in that area.

Pupils often get into arguments selecting team captains, and some
pupils rarely get the opportunity to be captain. Suggest that pupils
follow this fast and impartial procedure. They should line up and ask a
willing non-participant to *face away* from the line and call out "odd" or
"even." If he calls "odd," the first, third, fifth, etc. in line step forward
and line up again (in the same or in different order). The rest are out.
The process is repeated until only two remain. These two become
captains and choose the teams. If three remain, he should call out
which of the three positions (right, middle, or left) is eliminated.
When umpires and referees are needed, they should be selected by the
teacher on duty since this will give them the authority they need to
function effectively.

Bad weather causes a special set of problems. Develop a list of
games and activities suited to classroom use or to a small corner in the
gymnasium. Actually, pupils enjoy many games that can be played in
or adapted to crowded conditions. A relay game in which participants
blow a ping pong ball ten feet is just as exciting as one in which they
run 100 feet. Volleyball can be played with a string for a net and a
balloon for a ball and players who can't move their feet while the ball
is in play. A tournament with five sets of Chinese Checkers can occupy
a class during play periods for an entire rainy week.

Snow that makes good snowballs is also good for snow sculpture.
Decide on a suitable subject in late fall and construct the basic framework of wood and wire. Store it so you can set it up with the first good
snow. If classes are busy packing snow around a framework, they'll be
less interested in packing snow around rocks.

In almost every group there are some children who continually
disrupt games played by others. When reported they usually protest
their innocence of any wrongdoing and claim they just wanted to play
along. Some of these pupils lack the skills to play successfully and some
seek attention through such behavior. You can begin to bring such

pupils to a level of acceptable behavior by playing with them and helping them develop physical and social skills they lack. Play catch or tetherball or marbles with them. If you make it look and sound like fun, you'll probably attract others and you can then involve them in the activity and gradually draw yourself out. A little help and advice quietly spread among several or even many such sessions during the year will accomplish much more than angry words and restrictive punishment.

Suggest that the entire class play together during play periods from time to time. Let them choose the activity and direct it. Games such as Pom Pom Pull Away, Hound and Hare, Dodge Ball, Flying Dutchman, and Three Deep are good large group games that are exciting but not overly competitive. A study of game books will reveal many other such games that pupils will enjoy playing.

School playgrounds should be arranged so that pupils can get off by themselves if they wish. Jumping pits, swings, skating areas, jump ropes, and places to sit allow pupils to practice skills or just sit and watch the passing scene. We have a tendency to think something is wrong with a person who wants to do nothing, and who wants to do it by himself. For a given child on a given day, that may be the best way for him to spend a play period.

CARRY OUT AN EXTENSIVE PROJECT

A play or operetta permits a group to move into a fantasy world of its own. Outsiders as spectators see only a glimpse of this world. Unfortunately, plays are usually given primarily for these outsiders. They should also be given for the cast and crew, because a properly produced class play can do much to unify a class and give it a sense of direction and accomplishment.

I can think of no experience as an elementary school teacher that gave as much a sense of accomplishment as the year-long projects of writing, producing, and presenting an extended play, operetta, or puppet show. The productions varied from year to year in approach and quality, but the warmth of the experience remained constant.

Consider seriously a dramatic project that would begin in September and culminate in May, a project that would bind you and your class into an unforgettable fantasy world of your own, a world apart from the world of arithmetic and spelling. It's a lot of work, but it's worth every bit of it.

Use the fall months to study your class and determine in your mind the general direction of the production. Give your class many opportunities to write, speak in front of the class, sing alone and in groups, and work with different art materials. Work with creative dramatics to develop dramatic imagination in pupils. Show your class how to study the melodic and harmonic structure of songs they learn in music class. Explain the form and style of the stories you read to them and that they read in their reading classes. All these should be normal activities in an elementary classroom. The difference is that you are also using these activities to find writers, actors, composers, singers, dancers, and set designers. By Christmas you should have a good indication of the ability of your class. If they're weak on writing ability, consider adapting an existing story to the stage. If they're very imaginative, consider developing your own play from your own plot. If they have a lot of musical and dancing ability, consider writing and producing an operetta. Let's assume the last possibility and follow the development of an operetta in an intermediate grade classroom.

Broach the subject shortly after the Christmas vacation. Ask your class if they would like to write and produce an operetta that they will give sometime in May. Generate enthusiasm but don't describe the entire project in detail. It's better to concentrate on only one step at a time. Pupils have difficulty sustaining interest in a five-month project, but they can remain interested in five one-month sub-projects.

Devote January to the selection of a story idea. Gather together a sizable collection of story anthologies, myths, fairy tales, and the like. Ask each pupil to read around in these books and select and summarize in a few sentences two stories that he thinks could be turned into a good play. Select a committee to study these synopses and report on the ten that seem to have the most promise. More detailed summaries of these should be given by the pupils who originally suggested them, and the class should then select three. The class should read and study each of these stories in more detail. Discuss the dramatic possibilities of each. Draw out ideas for adapting the story to the stage. Consider the number of characters in each story and any extraordinary production problems present. Finally, vote to select the one they will adapt and produce. If one or the other is patently impossible to do, remove it from consideration early. Level with them. Make such decisions any time you must. But when you let them decide, be willing to accept any decision they make.

For reasons that will become more evident when the play is being written, episodic stories adapt best. These are stories with one or two characters who have a series of adventures in search of some goal. Since each episode is complete in itself, the play can be written by a number of pupils, each working on one episode.

Note that most of the activity so far could well have taken place during Language Arts periods. Reading and discussing stories and writing synopses are perfectly legitimate ways to spend Language Arts periods. You will discover that most of the activities of this project can be correlated with your existing curriculum if you plan carefully. You will not have to slight your assigned curricular responsibilities.

Write the play in February. Begin by studying and discussing the form of the story and by outlining the sequence of major incidents on the chalkboard. Divide these into several scenes. You may have to omit some sections, add others, and revise the order of some, but that's all right. It's your play. Pupils generally enjoy this part of the production. Contributions may come slowly at first, but it's difficult to hold them back once the class catches the spirit of the story and begins to see it on the stage.

Do character studies of the people in the story. Discuss especially the main characters and how they would react to various situations. Drawing on creative dramatics techniques learned during the fall, do impromptu scenes with these characters in various situations related to the story. Ask pupils to write descriptions of the characters. Ask them to draw sketches of the characters.

Assign one of the scenes to each pupil. Or let him select his own. Ask him to develop that scene in more detail in narrative form. Then ask all the pupils who worked on each scene to work together as a group to form a plot sequence for their scene on the basis of the various ideas they had. Draw these together and discuss them with the class. Agree on changes where it seems advisable. Duplicate the plot summaries of these scenes and give a copy to each pupil.

Ask each pupil to write the scene he worked on in dialogue form. Read these carefully and then select several pupils who seem to show the most writing ability. Assign them the task of studying the various versions of the scenes submitted and rewriting them into a complete script. Give them a table in the rear of the room and release them from most other obligations for a week while they work on the script. Each can work on two or three scenes and they can work together on elements that run through the entire play. Work closely with them as your time allows. Ask questions that force them to constantly consider the dramatic development of the play. You will be able to see the finished product in your mind, but they will find it difficult to do this. Therefore, let them try out their ideas on the class by acting out pages of script they develop. It sounds impossible, but an imaginative group of intermediate grade pupils can produce a fairly good script in a week of such effort. Study their script and make editorial changes that are necessary.

Set it to music in March. As the class hears the script, it will suggest places where music can be inserted. The pupils who wrote the script will also have suggested such places. Agree on places where music would add to the play and then set the class to work on the lyrics. Ask them to write and submit poems that express the thoughts necessary to move the story along at those points. Study poetry and poetry construction in Language Arts classes during this period. Select the best lyrics from among those submitted. Write them on the board and work out the rhythm and measure bars together with the class. Duplicate these so that each line of the poem is set below staff lines and ask pupils to work on melody ideas for the poems. Let them try out their ideas on the piano, auto harp, tone bars, and tonettes that week. Things will be a bit noisy at times but the tunes will come in a week or so. Help pupils write the notes on the staff if they can't do it themselves. Select the best melodies. The chances are that this won't be too difficult as the best will be far better than the second best. Arrange these melodies for an orchestra composed of classroom rhythm and melodic instruments. If you need help, ask your music consultant for it. If you have pupils who are advanced piano students, their piano teachers will be happy to help them do some arranging.

I'm not much of a musician so I used to worry about this part of the production. I needn't have. It went easier than I would have imagined. There is more musical ability in most classrooms than we're aware of. Discover it and challenge it.

Put the operetta together in April. Sets and costumes will have to be designed and constructed, dances arranged, a cast, orchestra, and technical crew chosen. Plan your production so that everyone has a challenging job. This is one of the advantages of writing your own production. You can tailor it to your group.

This is a busy period. At this point, you will have to adjust your normal class schedule to rehearse the show. But because the group has worked so closely with the development of the show, you will not need nearly the rehearsal time most operettas require. Actually, just about everyone will know all the parts.

Give the operetta sometime in early May. I always preferred to give four performances over a two day period, three for pupils from other rooms during the day and one in the evening for parents and community. Children learn much from performing before several audiences. Their acting, singing, dancing, and stage presence improve considerably with each performance. And each successful performance welds them closer together as a group.

"My greatest thrill was to hear the music I wrote myself, and to hear the people clap because our operetta was good and not because they were our friends." This was the written evaluation of a sixth grade boy after one such experience. Children rarely have an opportunity to participate in something that is really good. A project such as this gives them that opportunity, and since it is a team effort, each pupil can take pride in the production, even the pupil who contributed very little. The length of the project welds the class together and gives continuity to the year.

The project should end on a note of evaluation. Plan your performances for Thursday and Friday if possible so that pupils can savor the heady feeling of success for a couple of days by themselves. And then make the production the first order of business Monday morning. Encourage pupils to view it critically in terms of its strengths and weaknesses, but end the evaluation on a positive note that will encourage them to continue their association with the creative muses begun so pleasantly during the preceding months.

7

AVOID BEHAVIOR
PROBLEMS

REFLECT ON THE NORMAL RUB
OF WORKING TOGETHER

Teachers are expected to establish and maintain good classroom behavior from the first day they meet their classes. Ideally, a class should develop its own system of restrictions, proceeding through discussion and experimentation until it reaches a consensus about what class members can and cannot do. Such a procedure would be impractical in most classrooms, though, because it would take too long to develop.

Therefore, teachers generally begin the year by outlining a framework for a social and authority structure under which they expect their class to operate. This framework is commonly called "the rules." A teacher may involve his class in the actual wording of the statements and in supplementary changes, but pupils generally see them as teacher imposed at first.

There is really nothing seriously wrong with this. Pupils understand that the teacher is expected to do this and that system and order from the first insure a smoother operation; they are generally interested in being a part of a smooth operation. They are also certainly aware of the rule structure under which schools have historically operated. Most school rules do not come as a surprise to them.

In the normal rub of living together in a classroom, friction between teachers and pupils and rules is bound to occur. Pupils will forget, ignore, or deliberately challenge the rules. Situations will arise that are not specifically covered in the rules. When these things happen, teachers must react if they are to maintain the authority they need to continue the room organization as they want it. This is the area of discipline or pupil control.

Pupils are generally willing to grant a wide zone of tolerance to teachers in their treatment of behavior infractions. They are acquainted with the common disciplinary methods teachers use, and they expect from experience that teachers will play the game fairly and match the severity of the punishment with the seriousness of the infraction. They don't normally expect to get sent to the principal's office for whispering during a study period. In my study involving almost 25,000 evaluations of common disciplinary treatments teachers use in reacting to classroom behavior annoyances, intermediate grade pupils considered the teachers' actions fair 73 per cent of the time.* This suggests that mature teachers can react almost instinctively to situations when pupils misbehave without fear of being considered unfair by their pupils.

A fair-minded mature teacher recognizes that petty classroom annoyances are part and parcel of his job, and he doesn't get excited about them. This is particularly true of those he can't do too much about, such as annoying behavior resulting from children's undeveloped muscular system. Young pupils will drop things and make noise because they are clumsy. An experienced teacher will understand that growth will take care of the problem, and if the action wasn't deliberate, he will recognize the occurrence with a joke or a grin and let it go at that. He will then adjust classroom activities so that such things are less apt to occur.

As the only mature person in your classroom, you are in an excellent position to show your class what a successful adult looks like through your handling of classroom behavior. When called upon a successful adult can establish fair and sensible rules by which he and others can

---

* Robert Sylwester, "Intermediate Grade Pupils' Opinions about Disciplinary Practices Teachers Commonly Employ in Meeting Classroom Behavior Annoyances" (Doctoral Dissertation, University of Oregon, 1961), p. 86.

live. He is willing to insist on compliance with this behavior framework when he must, even though it may at times make him unpopular with some pupils. And he will work for the early establishment of group and individually formed codes of conduct.

These are the tasks you face when dealing with pupil behavior. It is not in the spectacular and dramatic that a teacher shows his ability in human relations, but rather in the day-to-day handling of the normal rub of living together. Blend convictions, firmness, patience, and love together as you use traditional disciplinary measures teachers employ when two generations don't mesh together as they should.

CONSIDER PHYSICAL CONDITIONS THAT AFFECT BEHAVIOR

Some experienced elementary teachers insist they can forecast weather changes by observing their pupils carefully. They claim pupils are more restless a day or two before a major weather change. Regardless of the accuracy of their claims, physical conditions, including weather, do affect class behavior.

Pupils will react positively to a cheerful and attractive room that they feel is theirs. They will consider it theirs if they participate in decorating and arranging it. Time spent by pupils in such activities as arranging bulletin board displays and caring for plants is time well spent, even though the work may not be as well done as if you had done it yourself. Participation develops pride, and pupils who are proud of their room will tend to maintain it properly.

Color can affect the reactions of children. Classrooms are often painted light and neutral colors. Browns and greens seem popular because they wear well and are supposed to have a calming effect on people. Such neutral backgrounds are good if you use accent colors on them. Brighten your room with pieces of colorful construction paper placed on wall surfaces in pleasing designs (with Stik-Tak or masking tape). Change the designs frequently. Flowers also give a pleasing color accent to a room. Use a sign-up sheet if your school is located in a neighborhood where people grow flowers. Let pupils sign up for days or weeks when they can furnish flowers from their yards. Displays need not be elaborate. Even dry weeds can be arranged attractively in the winter. Have several containers available and let pupils arrange the flowers they bring. Keep room decorations tasteful. Overdecorated and cluttered rooms have a negative and disquieting effect on pupils.

Arrange your room if possible so that you have several semi-divided work areas. This will lessen distractions when such diverse activities as reading groups, individual study, committee meetings, and art activities are all going on at the same time.

If you have the space available, look around in second-hand stores for two or three cheap but comfortable upholstered chairs that are attractive or that can be made attractive. Or consider rocking chairs if you can find good ones. Set the chairs in a reading corner in your room and encourage pupils to use them when they want to or need to read undisturbed. Most school desks are not conducive to serious or extended reading and pupils so occupied often become irritated by the activity of other pupils. An inviting reading corner should eliminate some of this problem, although it may create another problem if everyone wants to use the chairs at once. Problems associated with a desire to use are always more desirable than problems arising from apathy and disinterest, however.

If space is at a premium in your room, change the desk arrangement and assignment frequently. Novelty will compensate some for too much proximity.

If you are bothered by a periodically noisy corridor, arrange desks so that pupils face away from that wall. If that's impossible because of window or chalkboard placement, consider a diagonal arrangement that will face pupils toward an opposite corner. Various horseshoe and circular arrangements also cut out outside distractions by focusing attention on a spot within the room and away from the noisy wall.

Note jarring, strident, and other unpleasant and annoying sounds. Most of these can be muffled somewhat or even eliminated if you work at it. Bits of felt placed between the object and the part of the room it touches often helps. You can regulate the volume of many classroom bells and buzzers. Loose screws and parts in mechanical equipment generally increase the noise they make. Plastic utensils make less noise than metal utensils. Desks that open from the top should have rubber stoppers on them and should be lowered gently. Pencils and other small objects should be placed in a small box that can be affixed with tape to the inside of front opening desks to cut down on objects dropping to the floor every time a book is pulled out. Ask pupils to fold rather than crumple paper destined for the wastebasket. Ask pupils to refrain from placing things on the floor by their desks where they can be kicked or stepped on. If you permit gum chewing, draw the line at bubble gum. Wear soft soled shoes. Each of these sounds in itself may not affect the noise level of the room very much, but added together they can raise it to the point where it gets annoying.

The temperature and humidity in a classroom can affect pupils' behavior considerably. There's not much you can do about the outside weather, but you do have some control over the weather inside. A temperature level of 72° or less is generally considered proper for a classroom, but you should also consider the size of your class, the size of your room, and the amount of sunlight coming into the room when you decide on a proper temperature. Discuss the problem with your class since teachers are typically so absorbed in their work that they are not affected by room temperatures the same way their pupils are. Consider seasonal changes and make adjustments when necessary. Assign the responsibility of maintaining the proper and agreed-on temperature to a pupil located near the thermostat.

If your school heating system doesn't have humidity control in it, you can add or decrease moisture somewhat through adjustments you make in the room. Most heating dealers will be happy to advise you on the best and easiest way to improve conditions in your room if you describe your room and the heating system your school uses. Sometimes a fan or a properly placed pan of water can do wonders. Your custodian may also be able to help.

Poor ventilation can also cause behavior problems, particularly if you have an active group of youngsters who tend to bathe infrequently. A stuffy, smelly classroom will irritate everyone in the room in time. Place short pieces of ribbon on incoming and outgoing air registers as a constant check that air is circulating properly. If it isn't, insist that you get fast service from your maintenance department. If the weather isn't too cold, bring in outside air through windows and doors whenever the class is out of the room for any length of time.

Most of the foregoing suggestions require relatively little effort and repay much in a quieter, pleasanter, and more attractive classroom that is more conducive to constructive activities than to misbehavior.

ANTICIPATE BEHAVIOR PROBLEMS

An observant teacher can spot many behavior problems before they occur. It's much better to deal with them then than after the behavior has disrupted instruction. Disruptive behavior is often a manifestation of one of the following mental or emotional states. (Learn to recognize them in their early stages and develop techniques for dealing with them.)

Boredom: This is commonly revealed through inattention, restlessness, day-dreaming, and playing with small objects. This behavior annoys teachers because of its implied criticism of the teacher's planning and performance. Teachers fear that the inattentive pupil will not learn what they are trying to teach, and that his behavior will spread to others. They are probably right.

If your pupils appear bored frequently, examine your lessons critically. If you've been trying to teach with minimal lesson preparation, swallow your pride and go back to your student teaching days and write out complete lesson plans, and then follow this procedure for a while with written self-evaluations of your classroom performance. If you don't have to write lesson plans anymore because you've been using the same ones for several years, and you have them memorized, have a bonfire and start over again. You've grown stale. Approach the subject differently for awhile.

Check your teaching by taping your lessons and replaying them after school. Note the time when pupils began to lose interest and try to identify factors that caused this loss of interest and attention. If you discover that you talk too much, involve your pupils more. If you've been reaching only a few pupils, vary your approach to attract discussion from the others. If you've been re-hashing material they already know, strike out into corollary areas that make them think about what they know. Make more use of audio-visual teaching materials. In short, don't try to rationalize boredom. Eradicate it.

Inattention can also come from poorly paced lessons that move too quickly or too slowly for pupils. If you move too slowly, pupils will have time to play around while they are waiting for you to proceed to something new. If you move too fast, pupils will get confused, give up, and dawdle or daydream. Select several brighter and slower pupils who are representative of the ability extremes in your room. Study them carefully and train yourself to recognize the subtle hints they give to speed up or slow down: a quizzical look, a finger idly doodling on the desk, a wrinkled brow, a lingering look out the window, less volunteered participation. If the class is proceeding too slowly for the brighter pupils and too fast for the slower pupils, involve the brighter ones in discussion, chalkboard, and explanatory activities that will challenge them and occupy their interest and yet permit the slower pupils more time to understand. Or give them a brief written question or problem to solve while you continue to work orally with those who need more time to understand.

In the beginning of the year note in your plan book the length of the attention span of your class in various types of activities. Examine these notations at the end of September and use your findings to establish a time framework within which you can normally plan your lessons.

Plan activities that will challenge children who complete assignments before the rest of the class. It's always a good idea to have some large class project, such as a mural or puppet play or model going to occupy the odd moments of such pupils. Or encourage pupils to plan and develop individual projects they can work on over a period of time, such as writing and illustrating a book, weaving on a loom, or making a diorama. Set up programmed material and individually viewed film-strips that correlate with current studies. Ask them to prepare bulletin board displays that introduce coming studies. Collect interesting and challenging puzzles geared to the ability level of your class. Write them on slips of paper and place them in a box. Encourage pupils to discover how many they can solve during a month or during the year.

It's not unusual to have a few pupils whose attention span and threshold for boredom is much lower than the rest of the class. Take their special needs into consideration without directing all instruction to them. Seat them towards the front where they won't be distracted so much, and where you will be able to observe their reactions more closely. Help them set up realistic goals they can meet in class participation. As they meet these, expand them until they can participate positively and actively during an entire lesson.

Class friction: Classes will occasionally split into factions. With boys, strongly competitive teams seem to cause this as much as anything else. You can spot it as they come in from the playground. Smoldering antagonism continues with flushed faces, mutterings, furtive notes, He-hit-me's and I-just-touched-him's as pupils move about the room. Limit or eliminate strongly competitive activities if your pupils can't live with competition. Concentrate on preparing them for it instead. Arrange activities so that pupils work together in many different and less competitive group arrangements. Insist that playground teams be matched in ability and re-organized at least weekly. Ask teams to agree in writing on ground rules if that becomes a problem. Frequently, one or two pupils cause much of this type of difficulty. While all pupils should referee playground games, these pupils should do it more frequently. They may become more tolerant of the decisions others make if they are placed in decision-making situations themselves. They also need to see how enjoyable team games can be when their type of player is removed from the game.

Girls frequently split into factions over real or imagined social snubs. They huddle in groups, speak scornfully of each other, cast withering looks, write notes, and ask to change desks if they are sitting too close to their current enemies. It's important to deal with this type of problem without a hint of favoritism, or you'll probably have to deal with some irate mothers too. When you note such behavior in its beginning stages, involve such pupils in some group project that will help others and get their minds off their petty jealousies. Get them busy on such projects as straightening up the school library, cleaning out and re-arranging the classroom shelves and drawers, or building a puppet stage or large paper-mache animal for the Kindergarten. Work with them and stress cooperative effort. Deal individually with pupils who seem responsible for such discord, who like and dislike too intensely. They need to have many opportunities to work closely with others and thus become more tolerant of the existence of others. Children who are allowed to hate do not grow up to be adults who love.

Room elections can lead to factionalism. Holding elections frequently and limiting the number of times a person can be elected to office during the year will lead to greater participation, and to less antagonism and disappointment because election to a class office won't carry the prestige it would if it occurs but once a year.

National elections, local issues, and religious differences can also lead to factions within your class. Anticipate these problems with discussions that study and compare the effects of tolerance and intolerance in group situations. Role playing activities can assist you greatly in your efforts. Ask pupils to develop their own code of conduct in anticipation of periods when controversial issues are being discussed and decided.

Anger between pupils: It's not unusual for two pupils to become angry with each other, or for a pupil to become angry at you. Anger between pupils can lead to fighting and the involvement of more pupils in the argument, and anger directed toward you can lead to impertinence and various attempts to "get even" with you.

Cool off pupils who are angry with each other. One way is to ask them to sit silently at the same table and write separate accounts of the events that led to the argument. Exchange papers and let them respond in writing to each other's accusations. Repeat the process for another round. At this point the whole affair will often become so ridiculous that the two will start laughing about it. If not, you can sit with them and let them talk their disagreement out.

Always go talk with a pupil who has become angry with you, whatever the reason. Don't let him go home at the end of the day until you have made an honest attempt to patch up the difference. It's never humiliating to admit error if you have made an error. If you don't feel responsible for the diagreement, you can still express sincere regrets for the disagreement.

Whatever action you take in cases of anger, open closed avenues of communication, the chief thing destroyed when people become angry. Communication in itself doesn't solve disagreements, but it's a necessary first step.

Withdrawal: Some pupils who are unsure of themselves, or who have experienced too much academic defeat, or who have difficulty making and keeping friends, withdraw from the group. These lonely children may compensate by concentrating on developing some solitary skill or hobby, or they may become apathetic and noncommunicative, or they may seek recognition through negative and aggressive behavior.

Regardless of how they respond to their problems, their primary need is positive recognition. You are in the best position to give it to them. They often don't want to be singled out for public attention, but they do treasure small kindnesses that point out their accomplishments. Recognize quietly their contributions to class activities, help they give you and other pupils, anything they have done to make themselves more attractive. Don't ever give them the impression you are too busy for them.

Let them get to know you as an easily approachable friendly teacher who is concerned about their happiness. Ask them to stay after school from time to time to help you with some classroom task suited to their strengths. In such situations they won't have to compete with other students. During these sessions talk with them about your youth and the fears and frustrations you experienced. Let them know of your successes and failures in dealing with problems similar to theirs. Don't overstate your case. If they like you they will be encouraged to continue working at their problems. Gradually lead them to an understanding of the universality of many of their problems and to possible solutions they can try. Don't hold out complete success and happiness as a goal. Most people must learn to accept and live with some unsatisfactory conditions of life that they cannot change. These conditions vary among people. A child may have a keen mind but come from a family in serious economic straits. Another may have an attractive personality but be physically handicapped. Work to develop the attitude that none of us should withdraw from active participation in society because of our limitations.

Study your pupils. Only through continuous and intensive study can you hope to discover the subtle changes in them that signal potential problems that will frustrate them and thus affect your work.

REACT WHEN MISBEHAVIOR OCCURS

Most teachers teach reading patiently. They realize that learning to read is a long process that requires much repeating and re-teaching on their part. They wouldn't think of punishing pupils who forget words and skills presented during reading periods.

Teaching proper behavior in school is also a long process that requires much patience. Pupils will forget or ignore school rules and good manners. You will have to re-teach proper behavior many times during the year—hopefully with the same patience you exhibit when you teach reading.

The first steps in re-teaching correct behavior are recognizing and reacting to improper behavior, just as the first steps in re-teaching reading skills are recognizing and correcting errors made. Pupils expect you to react to misbehavior if it disrupts the smooth operation of the classroom or the well-being of a pupil. Most prefer your firm maintenance of limits to the anarchy that would result from continuous indecisiveness on your part.

It's not enough to act decisively though. Your treatment of classroom misbehavior must be based on a mature consideration of several factors if it is to maintain good relations and guide pupils towards self-discipline: How will your treatment affect the smooth operation of the classroom and the psychological well-being of the pupils specifically involved? Should you call attention to or away from the pupils involved? Does the proposed treatment match the seriousness of the misbehavior? Should the treatment be carried out with the full knowledge of the class or on an individual basis? Are pupils who weren't involved in the infraction affected by the treatment?

Research studies have indicated that teachers' typical responses to misbehavior can be grouped into relatively few categories. A study found that 72 per cent of all responses intermediate grade teachers made to annoying classroom behavior could be grouped into four categories.* How effective and desirable are these measures?

Simple request: Teachers rely on this procedure for dealing with misbehavior more than on anything else, even though it isn't always

---

* Sylwester, "Pupils' Opinions about Teachers' Disciplinary Practices," p. 62.

effective. It's good that they do. A gentle reminder should always be the first step taken in the normal range of misbehavior, even with those who will not heed it. It is a positive nudge, one that draws the pupil towards you as a teacher rather than away from you as a judge, as the more severe measures do.

A simple request to stop misbehavior can take many forms. It can be a glance, the calling of a name, a brief pause in a presentation, ringing a desk bell. Regardless of the form you use, use it in the same spirit you correct a mispronounced word during a reading lesson. Employ it whenever necessary; direct it only to those who erred; make your request specific; and follow it with a brief explanation or discussion when it is in order to do so. Since nothing severe happens to the pupil you merely ask to behave, the effectiveness of this measure depends on the respect your class has for you. If pupils rarely respond to your use of this measure, begin a careful and critical examination of your relations with your class and of your expectations with regard to proper pupil behavior.

Scolding: When pupils do not respond to simple requests to behave, teachers frequently raise their voices and scold and threaten pupils. Such emotional outbursts rarely accomplish what teachers intend. Teachers who scold and threaten are as effective as barking dogs. Their warnings give pause the first few times you hear them, but they become progressively ineffective as the barking is repeated over and over. A teacher who scolds makes himself vulnerable in other ways too. He has a tendency to scold the whole class for the misdeeds of a few and thus antagonize those who behaved properly. He has a tendency to overstep and threaten action he will be loath to carry out when challenged. He has a tendency to make speech errors during his diatribe and the consequent smiles and snickers will just aggravate him further. There is a place for righteous wrath in the classroom, but use it sparingly.

Deprivation: Deprivation often goads adults to positive effort. We postpone the purchase of a new car until we can save the money to get at least a down payment. We spend Friday evening doing school work so that we can have the rest of the weekend free. Pupils also should learn that many desirable things in life will become available to them only after they have completed certain obligations.

Deprivation is most effective as a deterrent for misbehavior if it is stated positively rather than negatively, and if it comes as a natural consequence of misbehavior. Thus, you might say to a pupil who had frittered away much of his school day, "You may go home when you have completed your day's assignments. I would imagine you could do them in less than an hour if you get right to it," rather than, "You will have to stay after school for an hour because you didn't do your work." If a pupil shows that he can't or won't play properly in a game, it might be all right to deprive him of the right to play in that game, but it's questionable if he should be sent inside and deprived of his play period. It might be better to keep him active outside where he can work off his tensions than immobile inside where he will build them up. Tell him to run a few laps around the playground instead.

Occasionally, a teacher will deprive his class of some enjoyable school activity because of misbehavior during another. For example, pupils who are noisy during an arithmetic period are deprived of their art or physical education period. Such a practice is wrong. School work should not be used as punishment or to threaten punishment. Would such teachers deprive their classes of an arithmetic period if they were noisy during art? Popular subjects should not be used as bait to encourage good behavior. Rather, improve instruction in subjects pupils don't like and misbehavior will decrease during those periods.

Pupils who bring distracting toys and objects and play with them during school should be asked to place them in a box used for that purpose. They can retrieve their treasures during play periods, and they should take them home at the end of the day. Don't place such objects in your desk. It's too easy to get involved in petty accusations, such as that you take toys away from pupils to give to your children, or that you eat some of the candy and cracker jacks when no one is looking.

Removal: If a pupil's behavior is affected adversely by the particular place he occupies in the classroom, it is sometimes wise to move him elsewhere. Thus, a pupil who tends to annoy those near him should be moved to a place where he will be somewhat isolated from others. A pupil who needs much attention and help from you could be moved near your desk. Two pupils who distract each other should be moved to different parts of the room. A pupil with a cough should be moved so he faces away from the others, perhaps to the front of the room.

Removal should not be used unless it actually improves the situation and unless you do follow-up work on the cause of the problem. Some teachers send misbehaving pupils out into the hall. If the pupil can't behave in the classroom where the teacher can observe him, it's difficult to imagine how his behavior will improve out in the corridor where no one can watch him. Likewise, it's difficult to imagine how sending a child to the corner for not working will help him complete his assigned tasks.

At times it might be advisable to change the physical surroundings of a pupil to get his mind off something that is bothering him in the room or in anticipation of some behavior problem. Work out an arrangement with a teacher in another part of the building for such situations. Send the pupil to the other room to get or return a book. The change of pace is often enough to cool a pupil off if he is angry about something or to get his mind off some mischief brewing in his mind.

Extreme measures such as sending the pupil the office, suspension, and corporal punishment are justifiable only if the behavior involves a serious breach of school or community regulations, and only if you take the time later to repair the break in communication such extreme disciplinary measures usually cause.

Getting sent to the office removes a pupil from the scene of his problem and forces him to discuss his behavior with a third party. On the other hand, some pupils like the excitement of office activity and look upon such trips as a pleasant diversion from unpleasant classroom activities if their teachers send them down frequently. Accompany pupils to the office and present the problem unemotionally to the principal. When he has the information he needs, return to your classroom and keep your class occupied. Resist the temptation to moralize with them about the situation. Don't call attention to the offender when he returns. Begin overtures to resume a sound pupil-teacher relationship with him before he leaves at the end of the day.

It's also important to refrain from calling attention to pupils who were suspended from school for several days. Get them busy with something they enjoy doing, or at least that they don't dislike too much. This should remind them that school isn't all bad. Don't pile on missed assignments or say or do things that will direct the sympathy of the class their way. You will accomplish little as long as the pupil is angry with you and the school administration.

Corporal punishment can be effective but pupils think it's unfair because it's embarrassing. They feel that teachers should be able to deal with misbehavior without resorting to physical punishment. And they are probably correct. It's rarely wise to show extreme anger when you deal with misbehavior, and this is frequently the emotional state of a teacher who is administering corporal punishment. Stop the type of behavior that might require corporal punishment before it reaches that stage. The knowledge that you have the authority to administer corporal punishment is usually enough for pupils (if your school permits you the authority). Resist the temptation to use corporal punishment—but be careful to follow school regulations when you do use it.

DEAL KINDLY WITH SPECIAL PROBLEMS

Every pupil experiences frustration, but some experience it to a marked degree. In their inability to solve their problems through normal means, these pupils often develop their own unorthodox ways of dealing with them. The normal gentle means of restraint discussed above that guide and mold the average pupil are often ineffective with these atypical pupils.

If normal procedures don't accomplish what they should, don't use them. If you establish through everything you do and say that you do not think of your class as a collection of identical personalities, but rather as a collection of individuals in search of a group, you needn't fear serious repercussions from your class when you use special measures to shepherd your farthest straying sheep.

There are times when more stringent restraints will have to be put on a pupil whose behavior is currently antagonizing those who must live and work with him, or whose behavior is potentially damaging to himself. But always explain this to such children and balance such instances with others that reassure him that you genuinely like him. Don't deal with such pupils in anger. If one or both of you are emotionally disturbed, suggest that the two of you discuss the problem later when tempers have cooled.

As you work with these pupils, recognize in yourself biases you might have toward them. It's difficult to like all types of pupils equally well. You may be outgoing and prefer that kind of pupil, or you might be reserved and prefer that type of pupil. Neat teachers generally react favorably to neat pupils. A teacher who has lived with asthma is apt to be more sympathetic to an asthmatic pupil than a teacher who hasn't had asthma in his family. If you can accept the possibility of prejudice in yourself, and if you can accept the possibility that you also are not perfect, you will be more likely to accept your pupils for what they are. You will work with them to bring out what is good in them as individuals rather than attempt to remake them in your image of what they should be.

The atypical behavior pupil will exhibit one or more of the following characteristics to a marked degree. He:

- Cries too much
- Is overaggressive or too competitive in play
- Fights too much
- Is sullen and resentful towards teachers and schools
- Throws temper tantrums
- Is mean to younger and weaker pupils
- Uses profane and obscene language
- Will deface property and break equipment
- Is too eager to take a dare
- Is a tattle-tale
- Talks too much during school
- Does not complete assigned work, or if he does, he does it poorly
- Is too eager to show his (often superior) knowledge in school, and
- Antagonizes classmates with his condescending attitude toward them
- Wants to be with you all the time, or wants his mother to stay at school with him
- Gets too involved in puppy love situations

- Follows the suggestions of others too easily
- Plays alone all the time
- Daydreams too much
- Plays with children much younger or older than himself
- Is ill too frequently

While this list is long, you will usually have only a few pupils who exhibit these characteristics to a marked degree. Most pupils will be able to handle such problems with a little help from you, but these pupils need much help. Keep a daily log on them. Duplicate copies of the form illustrated in Figure 7. Keep a daily record on such pupils for the first two weeks of the month. Dispensing with the log for two weeks will give you an opportunity to return to it with a fresh look at the problem.

In recent years guidance and counseling services at the elementary and junior high school levels have increased to the point where most teachers are now able to draw on professional help in dealing with problems that go beyond their training and experience. Don't lull yourself into thinking that a course or two in psychology has qualified you to deal effectively with extreme deviations in behavior. These problems often stem from a matrix of conditions that may not be evident to you. Your training and experience have typically qualified you to do four things in such situations: 1. To gather as much pertinent information on such pupils as you can through case study techniques and through forms such as the one illustrated in Figure 7. 2. To administer "first aid" in the classroom when extreme behavior and interpersonal problems arise. 3. To seek qualified assistance from school and community psychological services and to pass on information you have gathered on the situation. 4. To follow the recommendations these people make on the basis of their study. Don't feel that seeking help in such situations implies that you are an inadequate teacher. Rather, the reverse is true. The inadequate teacher is one who doesn't recognize his own limitations and who considers himself qualified to deal with any problem that might arise in his classroom.

WORK TOWARD SELF-DISCIPLINE

Whatever procedure you employ in dealing with school behavior, work towards the development of self-discipline in your pupils. Don't

Name_____Date_____

Nature of the Problem:
1. Visible Evidence:

2. Possible Causes:

	Excellent	Normal	Poor
Group Acceptance	— —	— —	— —
Academic Status	— —	— —	— —
Home Conditions	— —	— —	— —
Self-Concept	— —	— —	— —
Acceptance of Others	— —	— —	— —
Health/Physical Condition	— —	— —	— —

Incidents that occurred today that hinder improvement:

Incidents that occurred today that improve the situation:

Additional knowledge gained on the causes of the problem:

Résumé of my relations with him today:

Plans for tomorrow:

Figure 7.

expect them to reach this goal during the year you work with them, however. Self-discipline is assumed in adults, but it is only hoped-for in children. A self-disciplined person is aware of and responsive to the wants and needs and rights of others. He can establish goals and work effectively towards them. He practices self-restraint without direction when it is appropriate. He uses common courtesies as a matter of course. It usually takes at least the entire period of formal schooling to develop these traits in people.

Formal training in self-discipline should begin as soon as pupils enter school. Each succeeding teacher should pick up where the last teacher left off and move pupils closer to a realization of the ability to direct their own lives. Expect forward steps to be balanced with some steps backward. But don't let these occasions discourage you so that you quit giving pupils opportunities to make decisions about their individual behavior.

One misconception that some teachers have is that they can develop self-discipline in their pupils by leaving the class alone for periods of time under the control of a pupil they appoint. This does not develop self-discipline. It merely substitutes a pale imitation of a teacher for the real thing. You can develop self-discipline in pupils by leaving them alone from time to time, but do it by really leaving them alone. Don't turn on the intercom to the office while you're gone, or appoint a pupil to take down names, or ask the teacher next door to step in every few minutes (although it's advisable to let them know you're gone).

Begin by stepping out of the room briefly while pupils are occupied with seat work. If your class continues working while you are gone, expand your operations beyond the other side of the door. When you leave your classroom, announce that you will be in the office or in the classroom next door for the next few minutes and then leave. As time goes on, leave the room while pupils are occupied with a variety of tasks in which not all are working at their desks. Finally, permit small groups of pupils to work on projects out of the classroom without supervision. If your class can do these things by the end of the year without prior statements and warnings from you about their behavior while you are gone, you will have moved your group forward significantly. This doesn't mean that you shouldn't discuss how they behave while you are out of the room. You should, but do it at times other than just before you leave or after you return. And, of course, you shouldn't stray far from your room unless you are pretty sure nothing untoward will occur during your absence.

A self-disciplined person can set individual goals for himself and stick to them. Ask pupils to set work goals for themselves as you begin a unit early in the school year. Say nothing to pupils about these goals until the day they are due. Some pupils will have completed their work on time as they said they would with no prodding from you. Give these pupils many other opportunities during the year to set goals and work undisturbed towards them. Work with the others to develop this ability. Help them set up individual assignment sheets that outline the work they should do during a day or week. Show them how to check off goals that have been reached. Discuss with them your methods of remembering and meeting the many and varied assignments and deadlines you face in your work. Show them your plan and appointment books.

Pupils will have most opportunities to develop self-discipline on the playground. By and large, pupils establish and organize their own games and activities with minimal direction from teachers, and so they must learn to share and cooperate if they want to enjoy their play periods. Look for evidences that your pupils are growing in self-discipline. Which pupils always want to be first? Which are overly concerned about whose turn it is and the length of turns? Which make excessive demands on the use of equipment?

If you have a number of pupils who seem unwilling to share and cooperate, develop games and activities that will encourage them to work together for the good of the team. With a little thought, you should be able to develop variations on the games that they like to play. For example, vary any standard relay game by adding this preliminary step: at a signal, ask teams to run to the starting line and arrange themselves in lines. A team can begin running the relay just as soon as it is lined up. The catch is, though, that the first person in line will not participate in the relay, but will stand aside when his team is lined up so that the second and succeeding players can run. If no one on the team is immediately willing to be first in line, that team is bound to lose as it wastes valuable time arguing the matter. After pupils have played the game several times, discuss with them the importance of sizing up situations immediately and acting in the best interests of the group. While the person who makes the sacrifice won't be able to run, he could be the reason for his team's victory.

Or play a variation on Dodge Ball in which the player who catches the ball has the option of throwing it himself or of making potential bonus points if he passes it to a teammate who throws the ball and hits someone on the other side.

As you establish situations in school and play that encourage pupils to consider the well-being of others in their actions and decisions, point out how each such experience of sharing and thinking of others helps them grow up to be mature self-disciplined adults. Even using good manners develops habits of mind that teach one to consider the welfare of others.

USE ROLE PLAYING TECHNIQUES

Moral and ethical issues are difficult to deal with in the classroom, because they appeal primarily to the will and not to the intellect. You don't have to develop strong emotional convictions about the six times table. You just learn the mathematical principles and facts and use them whenever it's necessary. But just knowing the facts about such things as honesty and prejudice isn't enough. You must also determine correct behavior in specific situations, and then you must be willing to act in accordance with your knowledge.

In this, hindsight is sometimes better than foresight. It's the answer to that age old question asked the morning after, "Why didn't I think of that last night?" Role playing is one technique that you can use to give pupils the opportunity to try out their responses in hypothetical situations similar to situations they face in real life, to stand off and see themselves as others see them, to place themselves in the positions of those affected by their decision and behavior.

Role playing can be carried out in several different ways. The technique described below is particularly effective with elementary and junior high school pupils. Begin by telling your class a story that describes a situation you want to discuss with them. Build the story to the point where a moral or ethical decision must be made. Stop the story at that point and let pupils take over and act out the rest of the story spontaneously. They may try out several endings and discuss and compare their reactions and their willingness to actually act as they decide they should act in similar situations. A story may develop as follows:

Bobby's mother had mentioned casually that she liked a pin she had seen in Johnson's Variety Store. Bobby decided to give it to her for her birthday which was only two weeks off. The next day he took the $2.50 that comprised his savings and went to the store. Mr. Johnson was busy in another part of the store, so Bobby found the pin himself. To his dismay he discovered that it cost $4.98. Acting on impulse, he looked around, slipped the pin into his pocket, walked over to the toy counter, picked up an airplane kit, carried it to the cash register, and gave Mr. Johnson a half dollar.

"Didn't you find what you wanted at the jewelry counter?" asked Mr. Johnson.

Bobby turned red and stammered, "No, I didn't," and started to walk away without picking up his eleven cents change.

"What did you put in your pocket?" asked Mr. Johnson suddenly. Bobby stopped, and the whole story came out in tears. When he was done, Mr. Johnson told him he could keep the pin and give it to his mother. But then he added, "I'll expect the $2.48 you still owe me within one week. I know you have a paper route and earn money. You shouldn't have to steal to get things you want. Now I want that money within one week, and no excuses either!" Bobby knew that he would collect $10 from his paper route that week, and he had just completed paying for his bicycle last month, so he wasn't worried. He was glad to get out of all this without his parents finding out about his attempted shoplifting.

But that evening his father asked if he could borrow his paper route earnings to help pay for some unexpected work he had to do on the car. He promised to repay Bobby within a month. Bobby was too scared to say that he needed some of the money, because his father might ask him why; so he agreed.

His mind was spinning as he went around to collect. He still hadn't figured out what to do when he came to Mrs. Green's house, the last house on his route. She certainly wasn't worth the few cents he made on her. She made him bring the paper around to the back door, and she was always asking him to mail letters for her and things like that, and she didn't even give him a Thank

You at Christmas. She was the richest lady in the neighborhood and the grumpiest.

"You around again?" she snorted as she answered the door. She got her purse, pulled out two bills from a big wad of bills, and thrust them in his hand. "Here's your two dollars. Give me my nickel change." He gave her the nickel, and she slammed the door.

Walking back to his bike he noticed that the top bill was a dollar, but that the bottom one was a five dollar bill. He hesitated for a moment—thought of how rich and mean she was, thought of how stealing was wrong and of his one attempt at stealing, thought of his mother's gift, and then . . .

At this point stop the story and ask your class what they think Bobby did. Select a volunteer to play Bobby and ask him to go out into the hall. While he is gone, select someone to play Mrs. Green and someone to play Mr. Johnson. Tell the person playing Mrs. Green to answer the door if Bobby comes back, take the five dollars, exchange it with a one dollar bill, and offer him a dime reward. Tell the person playing Mr. Johnson that if Bobby comes into the store with a five dollar bill, he should give him his change and remark, "Well, I hope you got the money honestly." Beyond that, ask them to act as the person they are playing would act. Suggest that the person playing Bobby should take the lead in any discussion. What they say should be based on what he says and on what they think the person they are playing would say. Then bring back the boy playing Bobby, point out where Mrs. Green's house and the Variety Store are, and let him go where he would go and say what he would say.

When we examine this technique we can identify seven steps. In the warm-up, you *prepare your class for the situation and tell the story.* Don't use stories that will harm certain pupils by presenting their loved ones in an unfavorable light, or lay them open to ridicule or embarrassment. Also, stay away from situations that pupils would be unable to solve in real life. Tell your class what you plan to do and what their part will be before you tell the story. As you tell the story be careful to relate it in such a way that names, places, and situations used do not point unfavorably to pupils in the room.

After you tell the story, *select the participants.* Don't select anyone against his will, and don't give anyone a role that is too closely and negatively identified with him in real life. Sometimes, as in the situation above, it is good to discuss the roles and prepare some or all of the participants for the parts they will play. Sometimes it's better to leave the situation completely unstructured, and let the pupils work it out themselves. Much will depend on the maturity and experience of the pupils, the specific roles being played, and the direction you want the enactment to follow. Note that in the situation above, Bobby was given no direction while the others were.

Then, *prepare the audience to observe alertly*. With groups using this technique for the first time, it is usually necessary to request them to refrain from any overt participation. Laughter and response from the audience will almost always ruin the mood you want to establish. Ask them to observe quietly so that they can discuss the proposed solution intelligently. Review the situation briefly and tell them what to look for.

Place the characters and *enact the drama*. Sometimes this will be a matter of only a few words. Other times the discussion might go on at great length. Stop the drama when the point has been made. Ask pupils to pretend that settings and props exist.

Discuss and evaluate the drama. Bring out strengths and weaknesses of the proposal. Did Bobby solve his problem by what he did? How do the characters playing the parts feel about it? Was the solution true to life? Did the pupils playing the parts feel comfortable in their portrayals? Could the problem be solved in a different way?

On the basis of this discussion *replay the drama and revise the roles*. Let other pupils try out solutions. Change the directions you give the characters. With each enactment, discuss and evaluate the solution proposed. Work toward a solution that seems best to the class.

From all this *develop generalizations*. Help pupils see the situation posed as merely a type of other similar situations. Draw out the moral and ethical principles involved in the situation and the problems associated with dealing with them effectively. While it is impossible to develop a specific solution to every problem of life, major principles of behavior can guide us toward proper action in most situations that arise.

Role playing is particularly useful in dealing with problems of prejudice, playground disagreements, classroom behavior, and after school activities. The situations you develop should indicate clearly the moral or ethical principle involved, and several solutions should be available for exploration. The situations should be close enough to life and of sufficient challenge to stimulate the imagination of the class. Seven additional situations are described briefly below to illustrate the variety of uses you can make of this technique. Develop these story outlines into complete stories that will be suitable for your class.

1. A pupil borrows another pupil's new jacket to go outside in the rain and get a book he left in his bicycle basket. While rushing out the door, he catches the sleeve on the door handle and tears it quite badly.
2. A pupil in another room misuses some playground equipment. Another pupil informs the teacher on duty who sends the first pupil to his classroom. He tells the pupil who told on him that he will get even with him after school.
3. Valentines are being passed out. A pupil opens an envelope with an unsigned valentine with an obscene message on it.
4. A pupil comes into the classroom during the noon hour to get his hat. The room is empty except for a fellow pupil who is walking toward the door from the direction of the teacher's desk. His desk is in another part of the room. The pupil walking out seems flustered.
5. A pupil had told jokes and made fun of another pupil who dressed and acted differently than the rest of the class. One day the two are sent on an errand to get something from the custodian. While they are waiting for the custodian to arrive, the "odd" pupil asks, "Why are you always poking fun at me?"
6. Several girls bring Barbie dolls to school one day and play with them during play periods. At the end of the day one is missing. Since they had put identical garments on the dolls, it's impossible to tell whose doll is missing.
7. A pupil who isn't a good player becomes captain of a flag football team for a week. He or his friends carry the ball on every play, and since they are not good players, their team is losing. The good players complain, but he replies that they never let the poor players carry the ball when they are captain, so the poor players have to carry it all the time when one of them becomes captain.

RECOGNIZE LIMITS IN
PUPIL-TEACHER RELATIONSHIPS

Even if you do a superior job of developing good classroom relationships, you can still have problems. If you're too good, your pupils might get to like you too much. And that can be a problem.

Be sure to maintain a clear pupil-teacher, child-adult relationship with your class as you work with them. The more successful you are in developing rapport with your class, the closer they will want to identify with you. Be friendly with your class, but don't become familiar with them. Seek respect as a successful adult and teacher. It's much more valuable than "pal" status. You have crossed the desk and are no longer one of them, even though you spend much time together. Watch especially the following areas of relationship.

Dress as an adult. Your casual clothes may be expensive, but they're still casual. Teaching is a profession, so dress as a professional at work. Avoid clothes that call attention to you. In this day of miracle fabrics, buy serviceable and attractive clothes that will see you through playground duty, art classes, field trips, and warm afternoons without giving the impression of a wilted petunia at 3:30.

Your school name begins with a Miss, Mrs., or Mr. Insist on it. They may have a nickname for you but don't let your pupils use it or your first name when they address you. The office of teacher is a dignified one. Keep it that way.

It's not unusual for a pupil to develop a crush on a well-liked teacher. Watch out! Look for the adoring eyes, the eagerness to be of help before and after school, the attempts to touch you. Be kind, but be firm. Show your love to all your pupils, but don't let it fall on one. You may be able to take such adoration emotionally, but the pupil can't if you return it. Maintain your adult reserve, even when dealing with such pupils. They'll get over it.

8

MAINTAIN GOOD COMMUNITY
AND STAFF RELATIONS

BE ETHICAL AND DISCREET IN FACULTY
LOUNGE AND SUPERMARKET

You will become privy to a lot of information about people during the school year. It's often difficult to know what to remember and what to forget, what to pass on to others and what to keep to yourself. Teachers who carelessly dispense information about others discover in time that such behavior redounds to their discredit. As you go about your work, learn to handle criticism, gossip, and classified information properly.

Criticism: It's been said that one of the difficulties with criticism is that any fool can engage in it, and that most fools do. Too often criticism arises and flourishes in secluded spots far removed from the person who is the subject of the criticism, and who is in the best position to do something about changing the situation. Be wary of such criticism. People who engage in it are frequently critical of almost everything and everybody. Note how quickly they change the subject when the person they're critical of (or a close friend of his) enters the room.

When you are confronted with criticism, such as when a parent is critical of another teacher, or when a teacher is critical of a fellow teacher or the principal, ask whether he has discussed it with the person involved. He should do that first. A person ought to have an opportunity to react to criticism before his critic airs it publicly. You would appreciate such consideration if the situations were reversed.

Use the same approach when you are on the receiving end of criticism. Go see those who have been critical of you, but who haven't shown you the courtesy of discussing their criticism with you. These people should learn how to work properly with others. They should answer such questions as, "I understand you have been critical of my work. Would you please tell me about it too?"

Don't become angry, sarcastic, or discourteous when talking with someone who has been critical of you, whether justly or unjustly. Recognize that there is a place for a legitimate difference of opinion in most actions people take. You won't convince your critic that you acted wisely if you shut off lines of communication by being rude.

Reduce parental criticism through a program of communication. Use the duplicating machine to let parents know what you are doing and why, whenever you do something out of the ordinary. If home visits in the fall are not possible, call parents on the phone after you've had a chance to get acquainted with their children. Ask them specific questions that will supplement information you already have. Use the phone to inquire about pupils when they are sick, to relate an interesting or humorous event that happened to a pupil, to clarify an incident you suspect will come home garbled. Send home samples of pupils' work that will communicate current school activities. Parents are less apt to be unjustly critical of teachers who appear to take a genuine interest in their children, and who have demonstrated that they are only a telephone call away when questions and problems arise.

Gossip: Don't engage in gossip. Don't listen to it. Don't spread it. Operate on the assumption that those who will gossip about others in your presence will gossip about you in others' presence. If you have a gossip or two on your faculty, steer any conversations you have with them away from personalities. In times of temptation recall the old adage: Great minds discuss issues, medium-sized minds discuss things, small minds discuss people, and infinitesimal minds discuss other people's weaknesses.

Classified information: Information that is given in confidence should remain in confidence. If you feel that such information should be passed on to others for moral or ethical reasons, discuss your feelings with the person involved. Try to get him to tell the proper person himself.

Information recorded in a pupil's files should be discussed only with professional people who need the information in the proper discharge of their duties. Parents have a right to this information also when they need it in the proper discharge of their duties, but you have a responsibility to communicate and interpret the information in a manner they can understand. This will vary from parent to parent.

Intelligence and achievement test results are two examples of information that parents generally want, but that teachers are often loath to give. You needn't worry about discussing test results if you do it properly.

It's generally better to stay away from IQ and grade level figures. If you must use figures, use percentiles. Be sure parents understand that the percentile figure given does not refer to the per cent of correct responses, but rather to the per cent of pupils whose performance their child equalled or surpassed. Also, be careful to describe the norm group on which the comparison was made. Otherwise a percentile is meaningless.

Better yet, present and interpret such information with Your-child-scores-like-pupils-who statements. Depending on the test or scores the complete statement might sound like this: "Your child scores like pupils who can read material written for high school pupils. You have probably noticed that he checks out library books that are somewhat advanced for a pupil his age." Or "You child scores like pupils who have difficulty with school. He will need considerable patience from both of us as he struggles with schoolwork that was easy for us when we were his age." Or "Your child scores like pupils who have a strong interest and ability in one field and do less well in others. Your child's obvious ability in science should be encouraged, but we should also use this to develop his interest and ability in other fields by showing him the relationship between science and other aspects of life. For example, we might tell him about Leonardo da Vinci's dual interests in art and invention."

Almost any time we meet parents, whether at P.T.A. meetings or in the supermarket, they ask the inevitable question, "How is my child doing?" If their child is not doing well, suggest a meeting at their convenience where the subject can be discussed properly, rather than going into an extended discussion under such unfavorable circumstances. When you meet parents informally, keep the discussion light. Tell them of humorous and interesting things children do in school, or better yet, show them you can carry on an intelligent conversation without talking shop.

Pupils will unwittingly disclose family secrets during Show-and-Tell time unless you take precautions to prevent this. Second grade and older pupils can write out the general topic they want to report on and turn this in prior to the period. First grade pupils can tell you about it beforehand when you make out a list of contributors. Stress frequently that topics should not include items their parents wouldn't want reported. Suggest they ask their parents when they are in doubt about an item.

WORK COOPERATIVELY WITH CO-WORKERS

People are more frequently dismissed from a position because they can't get along with their fellow workers than because they can't do the work required by the job. They often overestimate their significance and the significance of their position in the total program of the institution they serve, and they become frustrated when others see things differently.

Thus, a custodian may become irked at a teacher whose classroom is generally left dirtier than other classrooms. The teacher can't understand the custodian's ire because, "After all, that's what he's being paid to do. Without dirt, he'd be out of a job." The teacher feels his and his pupils' time during school is too valuable to be spent doing the custodian's work, and the custodian feels that the development of neatness is an important part of a child's education. Since the two can't agree on this aspect of a school's curriculum, their continued relationship as cooperating co-workers will probably deteriorate because both feel so strongly about the subject.

The task of the school is to educate children. All employees share in this responsibility though their specific assignments vary, and though they may define the task of the school differently. Since teachers constitute the largest single block of workers, and since they work most directly with the children, they bear a large responsibility for insuring a unified program of instruction. Consider especially your relationship as a teacher with the administration, with fellow teachers, and with non-certified personnel.

Administration: Someone has to be responsible for coordinating the efforts of all employees, for making decisions that are best made by one person, and for meeting people who have business with the school. When you accept an assignment to teach in a school, you accept the leadership of the administrators assigned to that school. This does not mean that administrators are infallible, but rather that you agree to work with them in the execution of your common responsibilities. You also accept decisions they are required to make, just as you expect them to back you up on classroom and playground decisions you are required to make.

Wise administrators will seek staff consensus on controversial issues and policies that they are not specifically directed to make. They will do this through committees, study groups, and staff meeting discussions. Take such responsibility seriously. If an administrator discovers that his staff isn't willing to spend a few minutes before or after school discussing matters of common concern, he may begin to make more and more school decisions himself.

The staff and administration should agree early in the school year on areas where the staff should be consulted before decisions are made, areas that are properly the administrator's responsibility, and areas that the staff would prefer to delegate to the administrator for expediency's sake. If issues not covered in these general guidelines develop during the year, the administrator should bring them to the attention of the staff for discussion. Guard your decision making rights jealously. Faculty meeting time is much better spent in such discussion than in hearing a succession of administrative reports.

Be friendly and cooperative with administrators. Theirs is a somewhat lonely task. A cheerful good morning, an invitation to visit your room when something special is going on, a professional attitude in dealing with teaching responsibilities and administrative matters, and a willing acceptance of the inevitability of reports and routine will go a long way to make their day happier, and yours too. You promote the best interests of the school when you speak well of them with pupils, parents, and their superiors. Cooperate with them so they can do their job better, and they will help you become a better teacher. If you can't honestly speak well of your administrator, you should consider asking for a transfer to another school. But don't undercut him.

Don't put on a show for your principal or for people from the central office when they visit. It's degrading for a professional person, and you will fool no one with your act, least of all your pupils and the person you're trying to impress. Any person who spends much time observing others work can spot an act a mile off. Be yourself. They expect some nervousness when they enter a room, and they allow for it in their evaluation of your work. They want to help you become a better teacher, but they can't if they don't see you as you really are.

Fellow-teachers: I can recall the acute embarrassment of a faculty at a P.T.A. meeting in which a parent commented on two misspellings in a report card sent home that day. One of the misspelled words occurred in a sentence that reported the poor spelling performance of his son. The guilty teacher wasn't identified, so all the teachers were suspect that evening (although they had their guilty colleague spotted before the parent sat down).

It's always a serious matter to embarrass your colleagues through gross incompetence, a serious breach of good manners, or a decision that gets the community into an uproar. If the roof thus falls in on you, you can ask to be transferred to another school (where your reputation will probably proceed you), or you can eat humble pie and never make the same mistake again. Fortunately, you are working in a profession with mature people who live with error and poor behavior all day long. They will forgive and forget if you demonstrate that you profit by mistakes you make.

Your faculty is stuck with each other, at least for nine months. You have to learn to get along with each other if you're going to work together as a team to carry out the goals of the school. Discuss all differences of opinion at a professional level, and have a friendly cup of coffee together after the discussion if you end up poles apart. Welcome differences of opinion because they force more careful consideration of the proposals suggested.

Vigorously chase away feelings of dislike, jealousy, and competition in your mind that center on "The Old Guard," the young attractive teachers, the teacher who teaches the section of your grade that all the pupils want to get into, the teacher who teaches only to bring a second check into the family coffers, the recently engaged teacher, the single career woman without a million family responsibilities every evening, or any of the many other teacher types who can best be described as someone you aren't but would like to be. A good faculty is made up of many types of teachers, each contributing what is uniquely his. Don't try to remake your colleagues in your image of what a teacher should be. Share with them what you have, and draw from them what you have to offer.

Go out of your way to be friendly and helpful to new teachers. Don't fill them in on all the unhappy aspects of work in your school however. Accent what is good and what is challenging, so that their first days and weeks are exciting. If you are a new teacher, go out of your way to be friendly and approachable to the older teachers on your staff. Don't hesitate to ask them for help and advice. Most people are flattered when others ask them for help.

Non-Certified personnel: The least effective way of getting something done fast by a cook, custodian, or secretary is to order it done. These people are busy. A conscientious custodian works as hard as you do, and he often puts in extra time just as you do. Be reasonable with your requests. If service is not what it should be, quietly ask your principal to look into it. It's not your responsibility to raise a ruckus about it.

Many people who accept a non-teaching position in a school do so because they like to work around children. They're usually a pleasant group to know. Get to know them as human beings and not as faceless minions. Seek them out when you begin work in a school and introduce yourself. In time you will discover they will gladly share their special interests and abilities with you and your class. You will discover in talking with them that they can add an interesting dimension to your view of the school since they see things from a different vantage point.

Insist that your pupils treat them with respect. Invite them into your room early in the year to discuss their work with your class. Raise their prestige with pupils by asking them to serve as resource people whenever possible in your class activities. Ask your children to remember them with class-made cards on birthdays and other occasions.

Be friendly with your invisible helpers too, the people who arrive after you've left for the day and who clean the room for tomorrow. A few cookies and a piece of cake left after a room party will be most appreciated. They'll show their appreciation too!

Get in the habit of commending special effort on the part of co-workers with memos of thanks directed to the person responsible, and with memos directed to their superiors. Anyone can say "Thanks," but it takes a bit more effort to write it down. A little extra effort on your part for a little extra effort on their part seems a fair trade.

PREPARE FOR SUBSTITUTE TEACHERS

It's a rare teacher who doesn't miss a day or so of school during the year. Whether you know days in advance you will be absent, or whether you get sick during the night, you owe it to your pupils and to your replacement to leave a situation he can step into easily. The substitute teacher is a versatile person, but his effectiveness is lowered every time something unexpected arises that could have been foreseen or prevented.

Discuss substitute teachers with your pupils early in the year. Intermediate and upper grade teachers can ask boys to relate difficulties they face when they substitute on their friends' paper routes. Emphasize the necessity for adhering to established routines on days when you are absent (just as a substitute paper boy is ill advised to take short cuts the regular carrier might take on occasion). If you have a scheduled pupil helper for each day, include special duties for him on the days a substitute is in the room. The helper could be responsible for taking roll, lunch count, and other routine duties you might normally do yourself. Days when you are absent are days that pupils can use to discover how far along they have gone in the development of self-discipline, how well they can carry on without your physical presence, and how courteous they can be to someone who has taken on the difficult assignment of filling in for you with little notice.

If you know several days in advance that you will be absent, adjust your scheduled work so that much of the day's work can be done with little guidance from the teacher. Review lessons, individual and group project work periods, tests, and one day projects are easiest for a substitute teacher to handle. Invite your substitute to sit in on your class the afternoon before so you can introduce him to your class, and discuss the next day's work after school. Adjust your schedule to take advantage of your substitute's strengths. This might mean that one period is extended and another dropped.

Most absences can't be predicted in advance. Therefore, you should always consider the possibility, when you leave in the afternoon, that you might not be back in the morning. You might be able to decipher chicken tracks in your plan book, but can a substitute? It doesn't take much additional effort to make your plan book understandable to any teacher who would look at it. Consider also the possibility that you might be out several days and always make your general plans for the entire week. Indicate time allotments. Include all information on scheduled films, filmstrips, and special activities and events that you might normally remember without a plan book notation. In short, include all information on the next day's schedule that you would want to have if you were the substitute.

Early in the year develop a file or folder for substitutes. Identify it as such and place it on top of your plan book at the end of each day. In addition to your name and phone number, include in it: 1. The current seating chart, 2. Reading and other groupings, 3. Statements describing routine procedures established for handling such things as room traffic, going to the restroom, handing out papers, playground rules, disciplinary measures commonly used, etc., 4. A copy of school regulations and fire drill procedures, 5. A description of your extra class responsibilities and duties for each day of the week, 6. A list of the pupils in your class with a capsule comment on each that would be of particular interest to a substitute, 7. Several lesson plans that a substitute could use if it appeared advisable to drop a lesson scheduled for the day. For example, it would not be advisable for a substitute to introduce a new social studies unit, or to take the middle lesson in a special three lesson series that required extensive preparation on the teacher's part. Develop lessons in several areas that you know your pupils will enjoy and that take minimal preparation from the substitute. Puzzle or game type reviews work well. 8. A form on which the substitute can describe the behavior of the class, special problems that arose and their disposition, and school work done.

CONDUCT WORTHWHILE
PARENT-TEACHER CONFERENCES

In recent years the parent-teacher conference has become a major avenue of communication between parents and schools. The P.T.A. should bring the two together, but not all parents respond to this opportunity. The parent-teacher conference succeeds in bringing parents into the classroom where they can discuss education as it affects them directly.

Parent-teacher conferences were first held on a fringe time basis in many schools. Teachers scheduled conferences after school and in the evenings. In recent years schools have begun to include conference time in the regular school day. For example, some schools set aside several consecutive afternoons at conference time; others set aside an afternoon every other week throughout the year. It's difficult to get fathers to come to afternoon conferences, though. One solution to the problem is to dismiss school on Friday and permit teachers to schedule conferences on Friday and/or Saturday at the convenience of parents so that both can attend if they wish.

Prepare properly for conferences: Conferences are commonly held in the fall after teachers have had a chance to get to know their pupils well. Some schools also schedule conferences in the spring. Begin preparations for the conference the first week of school. Collect representative samples of pupils' work and gather them in file folders or in large manila envelopes. Use the material collected on each pupil to illustrate your evaluation of his work, strengths and weaknesses, teaching problems you face, and the improvement shown through the weeks. During the days prior to the conferences ask pupils to write evaluative papers in which they summarize major learnings developed in the preceding weeks and illustrated in the day to day papers you collected.

Try to finish a unit about the time conferences are scheduled. Plan the unit so that much of the material studied can be displayed on bulletin boards and walls. Parents are typically most interested in the skills program of the school. Use these displays to point out many other important aspects of the school curriculum such as group projects, correlated art activities, individual research projects, notebooks, and discussion summaries.

Develop a display of books and materials you will use during the year. Include also scope and sequence charts that describe the breakdown of the year's work and the amount of time allotted to each part. Develop also charts that describe growth characteristics of children that age, and that indicate the specific objectives for the period being evaluated.

Parents are always interested in seeing pictures of and by their children. Ask your pupils to draw pictures of themselves by looking into mirrors, and then display all these pictures on a wall or bulletin board.

During the week before the conferences tape two or three minute segments with each pupil in the order in which the parents are scheduled. Ask the pupil to welcome his parents to his room and to tell them a little about the room and his work in it. You might also ask him to evaluate his work during the weeks preceding the parent-teacher conference.

If you schedule conferences in the spring, develop charts and graphs that describe class growth and achievement during the year. You will be able to draw much of this information from achievement test results. In this manner you can interpret test scores, show variation in the class, and compare class performance with national norms. It's often better to indicate a general area in a graph than to give parents specific achievement test scores.

Duplicate a form that you can fill out with the information you wish to discuss with parents. This form will serve a dual purpose of moving the conference along, and reducing the possibility that you will forget to include something important. It can also serve as a record of the conference if you add comments after the conference that include additional insight and information gained from the parents. Figure 8 illustrates such a form.

Send out an invitation to parents a few days before the conferences are scheduled. In this note indicate in a general way what will be discussed at the conferences.

Conduct the conference properly: Many parents are ill at ease when they step into their child's classroom. Perhaps they are embarrassed at the thought of a "public dissection" of their family's abilities. It's your job to put them at ease. The room displays suggested above can do much to accomplish this since they draw attention away from the individual pupil and to the work of the class as a unit. Parents should see their child as one of a sizable group of children learning together in an atmosphere where everything is geared to learning.

Use the pupil's picture and the taped segment to lead the parents into a discussion of their child. If possible, arrange three chairs around their child's desk so that his books will be readily available if needed. It's also less forbidding to sit there than it is to face each other across your desk.

Begin your discussion on a positive note. Tell a brief anecdote involving the pupil, or show them something clever or imaginative he wrote or drew. Use this to lead the discussion into your evaluation of the child's work. Call attention to the charts that show growth characteristics and objectives.

You might want to develop and give to parents a duplicated form similar to the one described in figure 8 so that parents can take notes during the conference if they wish. Often this information comes so fast that parents can't remember what you said after they get home. This is particularly true if they go to several conferences the same day.

Avoid technical jargon in your discussion of the pupil. This language, though common to professionals, raises barriers between teachers and parents. Parents may be hesitant to ask you to define the terms you use, and they may actually misinterpret what you say. Or they may hesitate to make suggestions because they feel they can't phrase them correctly. If you must use some uncommon technical words for expediency's sake, define them—but don't be condescending about it.

Name of Pupil_____ Date _____

Present: Mother_____ Father_____ Other_____

Opening Comment or Anecdote:

Communication Skills:

  Reading:

  Writing:

  Speaking:

  Language Development:

  Arithmetic:

Academic Studies:

  Social Studies:

  Science:

Creative Work:

  Art:

  Music:

Physical Development and Health:

Social Development:

Adjustment to School:

Special Needs in Terms of Total Profile of Pupil:

Suggestions for Implementing:

Figure 8.

Be a good listener. Stop talking any time it appears the parent wants to comment on something. Quite often they will come up with the same evaluation or solution to a problem you planned to suggest. It's always better if they can say it and you can agree with them rather than the other way around.

Be constructive throughout. Evaluate progress in terms of the future growth of the pupil. Indicate how you plan to use past performance to improve future work. Progress might be slower than you would like, but talk progress and not the lack of it. Suggest alternative solutions to the problems raised so they know you won't admit defeat if an approach doesn't bring the desired results.

If it becomes obvious that you cannot complete the conference in the time scheduled and other parents are waiting, suggest that the conference be continued as soon as possible, at their convenience, perhaps even at their home. It's rude to keep people waiting while you use their conference time to talk to other parents. Of course, a continued conference should be suggested only if the parents express serious concerns that can't be discussed in the time available, and not because you rambled needlessly in your presentation.

Summarize the conference before they leave. Review areas of agreement so there will be no misunderstanding. You may wish to add comments to your form after they leave, so it's wise to allow a few minutes between conferences. Walk to the door with parents and bid them a pleasant good-by.

COMMUNICATE CLEARLY
THROUGH REPORT CARDS

Most schools do not rely entirely on parent-teacher conferences to report pupils' progress. They also use some form of written report that is sent home three or four times a year. If it's difficult to summarize six to nine weeks of school activity during a half hour conference, imagine doing it with a handful of ABC's and checkmarks! Writing report cards is one of the most difficult tasks a conscientious teacher faces during the year. How can you weigh individual and class accomplishment, ability, effort, and interest and combine them into a single letter grade that adequately communicates your evaluation of the pupil's work?

Impossible? Not really. You make many such evaluations and decisions every day. Every time you buy a bar of soap you weight such factors as price, scent, color, and cleaning ability and make a single decision among many brands. If many people across the country weigh the various factors that go into the construction of a bar of soap the way you do, that company will make money.

While pupils and soap may have little in common, the principles of evaluation remain fairly constant. You have to know what you are looking for in the object being evaluated before you can decide whether it's there. When you begin a grading period, you should know specifically what you want your pupils to be able to do at the end of that period that they couldn't do at the beginning. Share these objectives with your pupils. Relate your lessons to them. Discuss collective and individual progress towards your goals frequently. Note how goals change from day to day. When a new topic is introduced, interest and effort are very important and successful performance isn't expected; when work on that topic is completed, successful performance may be almost the only thing considered. Report card grades summarize such changing conditions and needs.

In most cases you will use a report card adopted for all classrooms in your school district. It may be all that you would hope for in a report card, or it may fall far short of what you would like to use. Whether you like it or not, though, you'll have to work with it. And you can communicate with it if you're willing to work at it.

Begin with your pupils. Use the same grading system on their written work that you use in their report cards to familiarize them with your way of grading. Discuss with them what you consider in arriving at a grade, and how you weigh the things you consider. For example, if you consciously or unconsciously grade papers higher when they are neatly done, be honest enough to tell your pupils about it. Whether you should grade neatness in arithmetic papers isn't the question at the moment; it's a matter of informing them truthfully about what you do consider important.

Explain differences in subjects graded. A grade in spelling might represent the average score a pupil made on nine separate tests, while a grade in arithmetic might represent his ability to work a certain type of problem at the end of the period in which the skill was developed and may not consider the quality of the work done during earlier stages. A grade in social studies may include a pupil's ability to work effectively with others, while a grade in art may consider only the pupil's work without reference to the work his classmates did.

Grade papers together occasionally. Give pupils an opportunity to evaluate their own papers and the papers of their classmates. Help them set up criteria for grading the papers they grade.

Try to hand out report cards personally to pupils. Arrange the day so that pupils can work on individual and group projects during much of the day, thus freeing you for five minute conferences with each pupil. Show them the cards and discuss your evaluation with them. The grades they receive should not come as a surprise to them. If they do, you haven't thought of evaluation as an ongoing activity. Help pupils understand that the grades you give are your best judgment of the work they have done, and are not an absolute evaluation of their ability.

Most grading systems use one variation or another on a five point scale. Be sure your own interpretation of the scale your school uses is communicated to pupils and parents. Discuss your grading procedures with parents at parent-teacher conferences and at open house group conferences, or duplicate an expanded discussion of what you mean by each of the several steps used in your school's grading system. You might begin with the interpretation below and expand on that.

    A. Performance was uniformly excellent or it was at a very high level at the conclusion of the period evaluated. This pupil achieved all the major and minor goals of the study. (Identify such goals.) His level of achievement is much higher than that required to do advanced work.

    B. Performance was very satisfactory. It was better than the typical pupils' performance but not as good as the best pupils'. This pupil achieved all the major goals and many of the minor goals of the study. He should have little difficulty doing advanced work.

    C. Performance was satisfactory. It is acceptable in that the pupil achieved all the major goals, but not many of the minor ones. He should be able to do advanced work, but he might expect difficulty.

    D. Performance was poor. This pupil did not achieve all the

major goals of the study, and this will make advanced work even more difficult to do successfully. He is behind the majority of the class and will require individual remedial assistance to bring him to their level.

F. Performance was unsatisfactory. The level of work was so low that it is doubtful that this pupil will be able to do advanced work with any appreciable success. He should receive much individual help to bring him to a level where he can think of going on to advanced work.

Write a supplementary letter to parents of pupils whose work was poor, or whose work showed a decided drop. Indicate specific reasons why the grades were low or lower. Tell what you plan to do in the weeks ahead to help the pupil, and suggest what they can do also. End on a positive and encouraging note, pledging your efforts to help the pupil as much as you are able.

PART III: AT THE END

9

EVALUATE THE SCHOOL YEAR
MEANINGFULLY

A school's main task is to get rid of its pupils. Pupils leave a school when they have mastered those parts of the curriculum they couldn't handle successfully when they entered. April and May are key months for this annual housecleaning of pupils. During these months you will complete your direct responsibility with your share of the school's pupils. During these months you must evaluate the goals you established in September, the teaching you have done since that time, and your pupil's success in reaching the goals you established.

ASSIST PUPILS WHO
MOVE AWAY DURING THE YEAR

The end of the year comes early for some pupils. You can generally expect at least one or two to move away sometime during the school year. These pupils ought to have an opportunity to evaluate with you what they have done so far in the year, and to use this knowledge to move more smoothly into their new school's program.

Frequently a pupil's parents will know several weeks in advance what school their child will attend. Write the principal and describe the pupil's work to date in your room. List textbooks you use and units you have taught. Ask for suggestions that will help you prepare the pupil for a smooth transition into his new school. Perhaps the pupil's new classmates might agree to drop a note of welcome to ease the worry of being accepted into a new classroom. A friendly welcome signed by thirty prospective friends in a new community can do much to allay fears in the mind of an elementary school pupil. Messages and materials can be relayed so easily through school mail, if the pupil is just moving to another part of town, that it would be quite inconsiderate for a teacher not to use this means of communication to prepare a pupil for transfer to another school.

If a pupil is moving to a different city or state, encourage him to write to the Chamber of Commerce and ask for information on his new home town. Ask him to develop a class report and bulletin board display based on this material and on information he can get from library research. He should discover famous people who came from his new home town, famous landmarks, and other aspects of that community that will develop pride in his new home and anticipation for the move. Prepare him for a new life in a new community and shy away from anything that will perpetuate strong emotional ties for his present home town and thus make the move more difficult than it already is.

Spend some time with the pupil during his final days and draw together what he learned so far during the school year. Let him spend as much time as he needs to write a paper in which he describes and discusses what he has learned since September. Suggest that he include the following topics in his paper: Getting along with others, working alone and in groups, my language, numbers and measurement, the world and the people who live in it, the world and the plants and animals that live in it, the world and the energy that makes things move, art and music, physical education and recreation. Read his paper carefully. Note whether he writes about major generalizations you wanted to develop or about peripheral issues. Does he mention only things that occurred within the past few days and weeks, or does he summarize what he has learned during the entire school year to that time? Discuss his paper with him. Bring out important things he neglected to mention. Discuss ways in which he will be able to use his knowledge in his new school.

The last day should not be emotionally trying for a pupil who is moving away. It's important that you know the pupil's true feelings about the move. If he is anxious to make the move, it might be all right to encourage a gay "bon voyage" atmosphere and permit jokes and tricks played on the departing pupil. If he is unhappy about the move, however, keep him and his friends occupied with activities during the last few days. Always allow time for good-byes at the end of the last day, and bid him a genuine good-bye yourself.

Ask the departing pupil to write as soon as he knows his address. Despite their pleas of undying remembrance, the departing pupil and his former classmates will forget each other rapidly as they develop new interests and friendships. An exchange of letters is still desirable, though. When you hear from the pupil, ask your class to answer with a class letter in which they describe school activities that have occurred since he left. Individual pupils may want to add personal notes to the class letter.

Encourage close friends to continue the correspondence as long as they enjoy it. Letters are pleasant to write and receive when correspondents write about the little things in life that mean much to both, that permit the two to continue to share experiences though they are far apart physically. Discuss the joys and problems of such long distance friendships with your class. Use such occasions to encourage pupils to expand their range of friendships beyond their immediate neighborhood through correspondence with relatives, departed friends, and pen pals.

If you teach in a school where many pupils transfer in and out during the year, you may want to adapt some of the individual activities suggested above into group activities. Consider assigning bulletin board space to the topic of pupil transfers on a continuing basis. Depending on moving patterns, you can use a local, state, or national wall map to indicate where pupils came from and moved to during the year. Post correspondence received from departed pupils on the board. Display newspaper clippings that deal with mobility in our society. Use role playing activities to help pupils learn how to adjust to new neighborhoods and to meet new friends. Tell stories of explorers, pioneers, and missionaries who left home and friends to seek adventure and work in new places.

HELP YOUR PUPILS EVALUATE THEIR
YEAR MEANINGFULLY

End of the year evaluation programs are often guessing games in which pupils repeat bits and snatches of information they memorized. Think of evaluating as teaching. Plan your evaluation program in terms of its ability to teach. Test to summarize, to draw generalizations that give meaning to isolated facts, to observe changes in behavior that indicate real learning.

For example, suppose much of this year's arithmetic instruction dealt with the study of multiplication. Many teachers are satisfied if their pupils can work multiplication problems correctly. But if you want to discover how much they *really* know about multiplication, ask them to write a composition explaining what multiplication is all about. Note their answers. If most of your pupils answer in terms of how to work multiplication problems rather than in terms of what the process of multiplication is and why it is so significant in our lives, this may mean that you have emphasized the mechanical aspects of multiplication in your teaching rather than an understanding of the arithmetic principles and properties that are operative in multiplication.

Ask your pupils to bring magazine and newspaper clippings that deal with things they consider important in life. Note the response. Do most clippings emphasize war and crime trouble, or do pupils tend to bring optimistic clippings that deal with such things as the coming of spring and people helping each other? Does the response describe the relative emphasis you placed on various aspects of life in our contemporary society?

How much time do you waste talking during the day? After living and working together for seven months, routines should be well established. The class ought to be able to get through a day with a minimum of wasted effort on your part. Try it. Eliminate directions, questions, and comments that aren't absolutely necessary. Don't say it if a pupil can say it. Don't have a pupil say it if it isn't necessary for anyone to say it. Toward the end of the day discuss your experiment. How often did you have to remind pupils of procedures that should have been well established? How often were unnecessary questions asked?

Ask pupils to select a topic that interested them especially earlier in the year. Allow them time to study it in more depth and prepare a paper in which they report on their study. Study your class during this period. What topics do the pupils select? Are they excited about the opportunity to study again something they enjoyed studying earlier in the year? Do they get to the core of their subjects or do they concentrate on superficial aspects? Do they give evidence of making use of study and writing skills taught during the year? Are their reports vital and alive or dull and copied from encyclopedias?

Develop a questionnaire based on the objectives you established for your class last September. Restate your objectives in terms of behavior decisions. Ask your pupils how they would respond to the situations you describe and how they think their classmates would respond. Tabulate the responses and discuss your findings with the class. Let your class thus examine itself and measure its growth toward maturity and self-discipline. Below are directions and several behavior situations that illustrate such an evaluative instrument.

Boy_____   Girl_____

Read each story below. If you are a girl, change the word *he* to *she* whenever it occurs. Answer the questions below the story.

1. A new pupil enters your class. He isn't too well dressed and he doesn't seem to do very well in his school work. He isn't good at playing games either. He appears to be lonely.

What would you do?

What do you think most of your classmates would do?

What do you think is the right thing to do?

2. You were sick yesterday when the class had a test. Since you still can't go out and play during recess, you agree to take the test then. The teacher goes outside with the rest of the class. You

notice that your classmates' corrected papers are on the top of the teacher's desk when you go to sharpen your pencil.

What would you do?

What do you think most of your classmates would do?

What do you think is the right thing to do?

3. A substitute teacher asks the class to work some arithmetic problems she made up on the spur of the moment because she wasn't sure what your regular teacher wanted you to do in arithmetic that day. You are all pretty sure that the scores won't be entered in the teacher's grade book.

(Questions as above)

4. You are a member of a committee that has to give a report in class. One member of your committee acts like the boss and tries to tell everyone in the group what to do. The other members of the committee do what he tells them to do because they are good friends of his.

5. You and a large group of your friends want to play a game on part of the playground. When you get there you discover that five younger pupils are already using the area to play another game.

6. You are walking on the sidewalk in front of school when one of your friends calls you from across the street to come over. You are in the middle of the block, but no cars are coming. Safety patrol boys are at both corners.

7. You had an argument with several of your classmates and now they don't like you. You are willing to agree that you are partly wrong in the argument, but only partly wrong. They won't play with you and they are starting to tell lies and jokes about you.

8. Some windows were broken in the school over the weekend. Monday after school you overhear three older pupils talk about it. From what they say you are sure they did it.

9. You accidentally bumped into another pupil in the hall. He turns around and hits you.

ACCENT POSITIVE CHANGES THAT
OCCURRED IN THE GROUP

Something good must have happened. A conscientious teacher doesn't work for months with a class without accomplishing something. Savor those accomplishments, however meager they might be some years, during the last week of the school year. [Pupils want opportunities to show themselves and you how much they've grown. Let them. Let them take giant steps toward self-discipline where you have permitted only short steps during the year if you think they can do it. Let them discover freedom instead of restriction as they expand the limits of their minds and wills.]

Anarchy? No. No loving teacher will permit pupils to go beyond their ability to operate effectively. But no loving teacher will allow the year to end without probing the outer limits of their ability either.

As spring looms discuss with your class the best ways to make use of the knowledge and skill they gained during the year. Re-evaluate classroom rules. Dispense with those that aren't needed. Place an increasing burden on your class to be responsible for its own behavior. Begin with the assumption that a seven month maturation process has been going on. These pupils aren't the same pupils you met in September. You should have witnessed some positive transformation.

Spring is a good time for more social interaction. Plan enjoyable activities that weld the group together. If a park is located within walking distance, eat lunch there on occasion. Ask pupils to bring sack lunches. Number the sacks and draw slips of paper to determine who gets what sack. Or combine all the lunches into a pot-luck if your pupils lack a gambler's instinct. Plan activities that will interest the entire class during recess periods. Take a walking tour of the neighborhood with your class after school one day to see each pupil's home. Invite the group on a Sunday afternoon outing. Attend a Saturday performance of a local Junior Civic Theater children's play or even a motion picture that they've all talked about. Listen to your class as they talk of what interests them, and then use these interests to draw them closer together as a group.

Don't get caught up in the common spring error of issuing ultimatums. Occasionally a teacher will use a spring tradition such as a trip or outing to insure proper behavior by threatening to cancel it if the class misbehaves. Only too frequently, then, the class or part of the class commits the misbehavior and the teacher feels bound to carry out his threatened action. What could have been a fine unifying activity remembered with pleasure for years becomes a resented loss also remembered for years.

Print statements that relate to your year's behavior goals on slips of construction paper. Some of these might read, "We stand in line without shoving," "We respect the right of all to express opinions," "We play games fairly," "We obey all safety rules," and "We use good manners when we eat." Ask your class to help you decide where to place the slips of paper on a bulletin board under these titles:

How Well Do We Live Together?

We Do These All the Time	We Do These Most of the Time	We Do These Some of the Time

Move the slips of paper on the board as class behavior suggests during the spring weeks. Try to develop in your class an honest assessment of their behavior based on an awareness of the goals you would like them to reach during the year.

Spring days are good days to seek out brief periods of closeness with individual pupils. Seek out pupils as they are sitting off by themselves during a hot noon hour, as they are walking back to the classroom from play, when they are last to leave the room at the end of the day, whenever you find them alone with you for a few fleeting moments. Use these minutes wisely. Draw on your accumulated knowledge of the pupil and say something to encourage him. Compliment him. Tell him a joke you think he will enjoy. Ask him to do something responsible for you. Ask his advice. Make him feel important to you at that time in that place. Let him know you have come to value him as someone you can share whatever you shared with him.

If you kept a room diary through the year, review it during the last weeks. Abstract highlights of entries made early in the year. Pupils will enjoy hearing again things that happened to them when they were a young group. Relate especially incidents that describe problems no longer present in the group. Point out such growth to the group as evidence of their group maturation.

Give your pupils something to look forward to. Give them something to dream about. Let them think about fifteen years from now by pretending with them what they might be doing when they grow up. Dreaming is serious business in spring. It's a time for pupils to think far beyond the school year they are just completing. Help them see the year in the context of their future life. Paint with slightly rosy hues if you must, but give each of your pupils a dream. You should have at least one for each pupil by the end of March.

ENJOY THE LAST DAYS

Although you've been waiting for it all year, the last week seems to arrive suddenly, sometimes even catching you unprepared for it. It's a week that should be devoted to summarizing and reviewing the significant learnings of the year. It's a week that should be enjoyed because the group will reach its greatest maturity as a group during this week. Don't waste these precious hours on dreary and unchallenging activities. Don't end the year on a frantic note rushing to cover material that should have been introduced weeks earlier. Don't make your pupils' last remembrance of the year a week of housecleaning. Do make it exciting. Plan a few surprises on your class that will make them look forward to each day.

Many classrooms become a little unkempt and untidy by the time the last week rolls around. Teachers feel it's too late in the year to worry about it. Don't succumb to that kind of thinking. What good does it do to wait until the pupils have gone before you clean the room? If your classroom looks messy toward the end of the year, get into it over the weekend and give it a real cleaning. Toss out everything that has been cluttering up the room during the last weeks and months. Use water and a sponge wherever necessary. Make it sparkle that last Monday. Depending on the age of your class, you might even involve some of your pupils in this Saturday cleaning.

Re-arrange the desks to permit maximum class interaction during the last week. You should see each other and talk with each other. Arrange the desks so that pupils sit near their best friends if desirable.

Develop an attractive bulletin board display for your class the last week. Or you might consider a large display developed on an expanse of wall where all can see it. In this display review the year accenting the moments that have special meaning for the class. These may include references to trips the class took, parties they had, humorous incidents all enjoyed, honors won, things learned, skills mastered. Develop the display with a light touch. Poke a little fun at yourself in it.

Select a good book to read to your class the last week. Study it carefully so that your class will hear a good presentation of a piece of good literature as one of its last experiences in your room.

If at all possible arrange for a special trip during the last couple of weeks. This might be a good time to visit the local art gallery or a historical site. It should be a trip that is worthwhile for its own sake, and not just because it fits into a unit your class is studying.

Several weeks before the end of the year, divide the class into groups, one group for each school day in the last week. Ask each group to plan an entertainment for the rest of the class. It can be a skit, a puppet show, a new game, an in-the-room treasure hunt, a taped play, a musical show, or anything else the rest of the class would enjoy. Allow the last half hour of each day for the presentations.

Most textbooks end the year with review pages. Dress these up a little. Turn them into quiz games using the rules of popular TV shows. Use a spelling bee approach where possible. Let pupils correct their own work. Ask pupils to work arithmetic problems in their heads and only write down the answers. Write down answers and ask pupils to supply the questions. Divide the class into several groups. Ask each group to prepare a review for the rest of the class. Let your class quiz you to see if you know the answers.

You might consider spending an entire day on each area of the curriculum during the last week or so. For example, you would spend an entire day on science. During this day you would review and summarize the science you had studied during the year. You should plan class reports and group activities that make each such day interesting and challenging. At the end of the day collect textbooks and other materials that relate to that area of the curriculum. This approach has the added advantage of eliminating the furious last day rush to collect all the textbooks. More important, it unifies each area you teach.

Do something for the school or community to thank them for what they have done by educating the class during the past year. Your class might offer to clean up around the shrubbery. It might clean up a nearby park, paint a fence that needs painting, wash windows at a community tourist information center, or just promise to keep the sidewalks near the school clean.

Ask pupils to write an essay in which they summarize their thoughts on the past school year. Ask them to comment on things they enjoyed and things they didn't enjoy. In the event that you asked pupils to write a brief paper in September in which they outlined their hopes and plans for the year (See page 45), you can return these the last day and ask them to write their end-of-the-year reports on the back of their September papers.

Pupils in a class get to know each other quite well during the year. Ask each pupil to select a classmate and write a profile on him. Pupils should describe their classmates as they have come to know them. They should concentrate on personality rather than on outward appearance only. Ask them to relate interesting experiences they had with their classmates, things they have learned from them, ways in which they are better people for having known them.

You might want to ask your class to tape record a segment that you can play to your next year's class. Title it, "What We Learned about Our Teacher This Year," or "What You Should Know about the Fourth Grade," or something like that. Perhaps the class would want to discuss things they want to include and write them on the board. The narrators could speak from that outline. Perhaps the class would want a panel to carry on a free discussion. Perhaps each pupil will want to talk for a minute or so. Don't fear a little gentle ribbing aimed your way. Your next class will discover through it that you don't take yourself so seriously that your pupils can't joke with you.

Plan a busy day the last day. Keep pupils occupied with special lessons that are challenging in themselves. Pupils know that last day activities have no grading implication. Don't pretend they do. End the day with a brief review of the year and a sincere good-bye. Each pupil might want to tell his summer's plans and you should too. Shake hands with them as they leave. Have a special parting comment for each pupil.

COMPLETE THE YEAR PROMPTLY
AND LOOK FORWARD TO THE NEXT

Closing up shop at the end of the year is only as difficult and depressing as you make it. If you wait until your pupils are gone before you begin the task, it will be difficult. If you begin your preparations several weeks before the end of the year, you will find that you can complete many of your responsibilities within your normal work days.

The largest and most important task you face is that of completing entries in pupils' cumulative folders. Normally, quite a bit of information will be enclosed in these folders, much of it on assorted pieces of paper placed in the files during the year. It will take you two or three days to summarize the information and evaluations and to enter them into the records if you wait until the school year is over. Begin instead two or three weeks before the end of the school year. Select two or three pupils each day and study their folders carefully the evening before. Pay particular attention to them during the next day and make pencil entries in their records after school. It won't take more than an hour or two to make all entries permanent after the school year is over. The pencil entries permit last minute changes you might want to make.

Take the time to give your pupils' next teachers the help you would have appreciated last September. The easiest way to do this is to staple together and place in each pupil's file several pieces of information, an autobiography written by the pupil at the end of the year, samples of the pupil's work and particularly samples that illustrate problem areas, and a page in which you expand somewhat on file entries you made. You should comment especially on any major changes from the entries of the year before and suggest reasons for the improvement or regression. You should also comment on the pupil's strengths and weaknesses, on any social problems he might have, and on your relationships with his parents.

A report card is generally a rather impersonal thing. As you complete the records of each pupil, take the time to write a brief note to his parents. It takes but a few minutes to express your appreciation for the responsibility they entrusted to you. Whether their child was a joy or a problem to teach, he did provide part of your livelihood during the year. Write a few genuine words in parting that will encourage the parents in the task they still face and that will give more guidance to them than they will get from your check marks and letter grades on the report card. Such concern for pupils beyond contractual obligations will do much to increase the confidence parents place in schools.

School policies regarding your end-of-the-year responsibilities should be taken seriously. It's not to the credit of the teaching profession that many school districts hold up pay checks until classrooms are arranged as required and keys are turned into the office. The money a school district can save on efficient administration and maintenance is available for instructional expenditures. The amount you save your school by careful attention to your contractual and ethical obligations may be slight, but your example encourages other staff members to do the same, and the total savings may be substantial. Don't look down your nose at combining two partially filled cans of yellow tempera to make an almost full can for next September's storeroom. It's easier to toss the cans in the garbage can, but it's not the right thing to do.

Make an effort to get acquainted with next year's class if at all possible before the end of the school year. If your school situation is such that you know which group of pupils will enter your room in the fall, get together with their teacher and arrange things so that you can see and work with the group in action. It's usually not difficult to work the two classes together in recreational and physical education activities. Through shared supervision of such periods you can learn much about the interpersonal relationships that exist in the class. Invite the class into your room several times during the spring to view skits your pupils develop in connection with units you teach. With a little effort you can learn the names of many of them during the spring weeks. Greet them by name whenever you meet them.

Keep in touch with your former pupils. If you take a trip during the summer, send them all a card from the place on your trip that you think would interest them most. The small expenditure in time and money this gesture demands is more than amply repaid by the results it brings. Your pupils will know that you didn't have to do it; it isn't a part of your job. It can only mean that you really did care for them, that you really enjoyed knowing them and working with them. If you spend the summer at home, ask your class to consider a park party if it's possible sometime during the summer. If it isn't, make an effort to stop by the community parks your pupils use several times during the summer to say hello and pass the time of day with them.

Since many pupils take trips during the summer, ask all pupils who are interested to bring a stamped envelope with their 4th of July address on it. Place the envelopes in a box and ask each pupil involved to draw one out. On July 4th the pupils should write a letter to the classmate whose envelope they have. They should tell about their summer adventures and anything else they think will interest their classmate.

Ask your pupils to look into the future and guess what they will be doing when they are twenty-five years old. Collect their papers and place them in a large envelope. Suggest that they write to you on their twenty-fifth birthday and tell you what has happened to them in the intervening years. Promise to return their school prophecy by return mail. Give them an address where you are sure you can be reached years from now, where mail can be forwarded if necessary. Suggest that pupils place the address in their wallets. You might be surprised at the number of letters you will get, and at which pupils write. More important, every time pupils run across your address as they hunt through their wallets for something in the years ahead, they will remember you, and whenever they remember you, they will remember what you taught them during the short period you worked together.

Life becomes richer as we grow older because pleasant memories occupy more and more of our thoughts. It's worth the effort to work hard at your teaching so that at least some of your pupils' future pleasant memories will be of the year they got to know you as their teacher.

INDEX

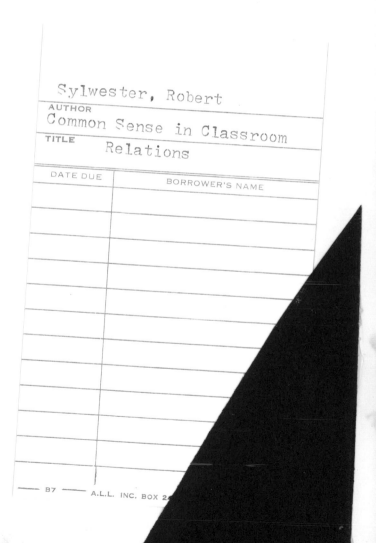

Sylwester, Robert
AUTHOR
Common Sense in Classroom
TITLE   Relations

DATE DUE	BORROWER'S NAME